# DAVIE COUNTY MAVERICKS

# DAVIE COUNTY MAVERICKS

## *Four Men Who Changed History*

MARCIA D. PHILLIPS

THE History PRESS

Published by The History Press
Charleston, SC
www.historypress.net



*Front cover, bottom, and back cover, courtesy of Stephen Phillips.*

First published 2018

Manufactured in the United States

ISBN 9781467139557

Library of Congress Control Number: 2017963224

*This book is lovingly dedicated to*
*Three boys growing up in this century*

*Clive Wilson*
*Job Wilson*
*Caden Phillips*

*my grandsons who will find themselves in this book*
*and whose courage will lead them to make their own contributions in life*

*History doesn't repeat itself*
*But it often rhymes.*
*—Attributed to Mark Twain*

# CONTENTS

# Acknowledgements

No one writes a book entirely alone, although it can seem that way in early morning wrestling matches with words. I owe what is right about this book to the following, and any lack is my responsibility alone.

I am thankful to the generous people of Davie County, especially my relatives, who gave me a place to call home when growing up and welcomed me back five years ago. I believe they deserve to have their rich history written.

The Davie County Public Library, the first library I fell in love with, created a history room of resources and generously made them available to novice and historian alike. From Director Jane McAllister to the workers who kindly, repeatedly unlocked cases for me, they were nothing but helpful and supportive. Local historians were a great source of information, including the late James Wall, Randell Jones, Marie Craig and my cousin Rex Bowers, the most knowledgeable local historian I know because he has walked every inch in Davie County. Maxine Ferebee Pruitt was also generous with her time and family stories. I have learned much from my colleagues at Old Salem. Thank you to all.

The staff members of the North Carolina Museum of History, the Museum of Early Southern Decorative Arts in Old Salem, Piedmont International University Library, Davidson College Special Collections, the Wilson Special Collections Library at UNC in Chapel Hill, Fort Dobbs, the National Archives and the 509th Composite Group helped me secure images.

A special thanks to my photographer and son Stephen Phillips for capturing the modern images so superbly.

I appreciate The History Press for their commitment to publish local history in small markets. My acquisitions editor, Kate Jenkins, and senior editor Hilary Parrish were a great help in this process.

My family contributes so much to my personal life story. My mother, Dorothy Boger, gave me deep Davie County roots and much encouragement. I owe much to my dad, George Dollar, who was an outstanding historian, and to my four children, Annalisa, Nathan, Susanna and Stephen, who not only listened to my history stories growing up but now inspire me daily with their own courageous spirits.

My husband, Bill Phillips, brought me back home even while giving me one for forty years. Home is not just a place but a person.

# Introduction

History consists of stories. Stories consist of settings, plots and characters. Readers may know the setting, will discover the plot as it unfolds and hopefully come to feel as if they have met the characters. Unlike fiction, historical stories tell of real events, and sometimes the perception is that they are not as dramatic. But real history has its own drama—human drama—and facts truly are stranger, and usually much more interesting, than fiction.

This book attempts to tell a few true stories. It is not intended to be a comprehensive biography of any of the three men from Davie County—Daniel Boone, the legendary explorer of the West; Hinton Helper, whose controversial book on slavery in the South fueled the Civil War; and Thomas Ferebee, the bombardier of the *Enola Gay*—or the fourth, Peter Ney, who lived the end of his life here. Neither is this a groundbreaking work revealing new historical information. The facts presented here fall in the realm of public knowledge. Nor is it exhaustive. Much more can be learned and revealed about these lives, and it is hoped this book will cause that hidden information to surface, as books so often do. Rather, this work is intended to be a sketch of how four lives intersected in one way only—on the same small spot of land—and how that land nourished their dreams and very different individual futures in similar ways.

Big stories often have their beginnings in small places. Most historical stories focus on the events or people as the key players, and the land shows up in incidental mention. The exception to this is extreme landscapes or climates, but all places have uniqueness to them, and the lives and events that play out in that place are shaped by it. Individuals are molded by many factors, mostly genetics and the influence of others, but the environment of development should not be ignored in its importance. This is not a geography book, but the geography in this collection of stories does more than just show up in passing; it is a determining factor in the creation of famous men. It is the fifth character in this book. Three young men grew into themselves in this small place, this rural countryside in Davie County. If geography is too boring for the reader, he should skip the first two chapters. But these chapters really should not be skipped. Give geography a chance to be interesting. It gives context and perspective to what otherwise appear to be random events. It is the tie that binds these lives together.

Also included are additional informational tidbits that can appear at first to not be connected to Davie County, but just the opposite is true. Unique as this place is, it shares similarities and connections to other parts of the world and world history. What connects a small place to the greater story of mankind is stronger than what separates them.

These particular stories took place near the present-day town of Mocksville in Davie County, North Carolina. Located in the western Piedmont of the state, Davie County has a distinctive identity as a county. There are four towns and many more small communities but no cities within its borders. It is rural, proudly country in its lifestyle, conservative and traditional. There exists among longtime residents a deep-seated loyalty to the place. Unlike most Americans, residents here identify themselves as being from Davie County and not a certain town. It is a beautiful and peaceful rural place with a strong sense of belonging for its residents.

The central characters in this book are three young men who grew up along the banks of Bear Creek hunting, fishing and dreaming. None of the three primary historical figures ever met each other, nor could they have within their lifetimes. They were born in three different centuries and lived in three very different eras: the colonial age of exploration, the Industrial Revolution and the modern global era. Yet they became significant figures at turning points in American history in radically different ways—one with his hand on a musket, the next with a pen and the third with a handle to pull. History was indeed in their hands. The fourth Mystery Man merely showed up, literally, and lived out his final years here (unlike the other three). Yet in addition to greatly influencing one of the boys and serving as a stark contrast to these three rural North Carolina youths, he also is a great example of how the place where a person's story begins never ceases to be a factor in his life.

Here is the place in Davie County and some of its best stories.

*Chapter 1*

# History's Place

History does not take place in a vacuum. It happens in a physical place where there is dirt and sky and water and animals and plants and sometimes humans, but they generally come into the place last. This place is a natural setting where anything can happen or nothing may happen. Sometimes the dirt gets to serve as a stage, a backdrop for human drama, but it is just a geographical place before it becomes a location for history to happen and later perhaps a famous name in books. Long before a monument or sign is erected, it is just a piece of dirt, a place of earth surrounded by more dirt. But then something special takes place at that spot and not at any other place. It might change the place forever, and a city grows there or it becomes a national park eventually. Other times, nothing much changes and the history makers move on, and the earth is left with no indication of its brush with history. But there is always a place where a story begins or has a turning point or ends. History cannot happen without that. History has to have a place where it happens.

Why does history happen where it does? Why was Stonehenge built where it was? Why did Alexander's army and his empire quit conquering more and more land where it did? Why did Egyptian civilization develop mostly along the banks of the Nile River? Why did the Pilgrims settle in Massachusetts and not farther south in Virginia?

Experts are still not in total agreement about Stonehenge, which is just the most famous of a number of such ancient stone circles in England, but it seems it was a burial ground, so no doubt its location began as simply where someone died. Alexander took his troops too far from home, dealt with resistance and revolt and then died unexpectedly; the place was where he ran out of luck and time. The Nile River was a source of life-sustaining water in the Sahara Desert. The Pilgrims were blown farther north than they intended and so settled in present-day New England. Death, distance, water and wind are the answers to those questions.

Obviously, the human factors of will, choice and ambition play a large part in where history happens, but what about the role of the place itself? What about the place made it *the* place and not another?

History happens where it does for a reason. So many factors contribute to the unique nature of a place—location, type of soil, topography, climate, proximity to a water source, native plant life, native animal life—and the list goes on to lesser factors. But in many cases, the physical stage is more than just a backdrop to the events that unfold; it is also a force of causation, the reason certain dynamics develop into strong people and actions and unique results. What happens in one place at one time may resemble events in another place and time, but they are never exactly the same. This difference is mostly driven by the people who participate and the choices they make, but they are first shaped by the resources and constraints of the surrounding environment. This may look like positive influence but also may manifest as obstacles to be overcome.

The soil that supports life (and not all land does), the river that provides life-sustaining water and a travel route, the woods that give timber for shelter and animals for food and a climate that is not prohibitively challenging all make a place livable to the first humans to arrive there. The lay of the land, such as flat and open for farming or sloping away from a creek in a natural water system, allows for humans to gather in a community and determines how they live off the land. People have always followed water and generally chosen good land. As far back as the biblical Old Testament, ancient records show migrations driven by the place that supports life; the first inhabited land in the book of Genesis was identified by the names of the four rivers. The Hebrew people were encouraged in Psalm 1:3 in the Bible to thrive like trees planted by streams of water.

A place's location, such as where two natural paths intersected, gave rise to settlements for convenience of trade. People groups, with more primitive means of transportation than today, like water, often followed the path of least resistance. For instance, the Great Wagon Road did not go along the peaks of the Appalachian Mountain Range (where roads like the Blue Ridge Parkway do today) but across the foothills, where it was much easier to walk and to lead horse-drawn wagons. Even what seemed like an accident of location—like the Battle of Gettysburg, where the two armies simply encountered each other—happened where it did because people had developed a system of movement that led the troops there. Those systems were based on something in the environment that had motivated walkers to travel that route in the first place. The roads that took them there reflected the natural conditions that made footpaths possible, which then became horse trails and later wagon roads. Today's highways are usually built where the physical environment allowed a Native American to first wander.

Mountains have most often acted as barriers in history. The Himalayans kept the Indian peninsula isolated and thus a subcontinent (larger than most peninsulas but not quite big enough for geographers to identify as a separate continent), and a unique culture developed there. The Alps allowed the Swiss to maintain neutrality in most of Europe's conflicts until the era of aviation greatly altered the ability of that natural fortress to protect them. The Appalachian Mountain Range kept the British colonists concentrated along the Eastern Seaboard, and only because of this were the thirteen colonies able to work together and successfully fight the American Revolutionary War against England. Mountains even impact weather in a region by blocking fronts or creating a climate shelf on lower ground.

Weather always impacts a place and history. In the modern era, when humans can insulate themselves from the elements, it would be a huge mistake to ignore that those same elements of weather originally shaped the actions that gave rise to the present. Even today there are places on the earth that are uninhabitable because of weather alone. Antarctica and deserts come to mind (which, incidentally, since the term *desert* identifies a place not according to its heat but its low annual precipitation, technically Antarctica is the largest desert on earth). So humans settled where they had the knowledge and skills to survive the most extreme weather conditions in that particular place.

Many an exodus (like the Old Testament book of the same name, this refers to a mass movement of people as a group, from the Greek word for which the English language gets the word "exit") resulted when people could not survive a particular place. Most people know of the famous reasons, such as political or religious motivation, but others included the push or the pull of the environment that drove them to move on, as shepherds still do today as they have for thousands of years to find new pastures for their herds.

Historic buildings, particularly those built for human shelter, reflect this need to create a way to survive the local climate. In New England, houses were built with the chimney in the center of the house for cooking but also to provide warmth against the winter's bitter cold. In the South, chimneys for cooking fireplaces were built on outside walls (or even in a separate kitchen) and on the periphery of the house to limit heat in the hot summers. Today's homes with central heating and air conditioning do not reflect this as much.

In a modern culture when houses are built from a predetermined pattern with any material desired, it is easy to forget that the availability of raw materials such as timber and stone was necessary to make construction possible. Also, the houses had to meet basic physical needs of protection, not design dreams. America's iconic log cabins were a great example of quickly built shelters from a readily available resource: trees. The trees were simply there and available and could be made into shelter with simple hand tools. Other buildings were built according to old-world notions, like the notion of the shrinking supply of forests and lumber in Europe as its population grew, which resulted in a style called half-timbered or Tudor where wood was used just for the skeletal support framework. The pioneers later switched to building log cabins due to a realization that trees were plentiful here.

Winston Churchill once noted that people shape their buildings and then the buildings shape them. This was true for most of history before professionals built standard buildings for others. Log cabins became the symbol of American rugged individualism that produced iconic figures like Abraham Lincoln. Communist leaders in Eastern Europe routinely tore down iconic landmarks and replaced them with drab, similar buildings as a deliberate attempt to erase a people's heritage. Modern generic structures often look like they could be found in any place and do not reflect the local region. What does that mean for this modern generation if buildings do indeed shape people?

Living near a natural source of water was an absolute necessity for most of history before modern infrastructures guaranteed a steady flow of life-sustaining water. Many biblical and other ancient references to water as a source of life indicate how important access to water was for early mankind. Water was necessary, of course, to drink for humans and their animals and to water the growth of plants for food. But bodies of water also provided a major means of transportation. While rivers divide pieces of land, they also provide a moving ribbon to connect with other pieces of land downstream. Rivers provide a visual channel by looking down the open space between the banks and seeing the world beyond you. Without water sources, humans would be not just thirsty and hungry but also isolated (and a lot dirtier). Not surprisingly, rivers have often become gathering places for everyone from traders to those attending camp meetings. Civilizations sprung up along the banks of rivers like the Nile and the shores of inland bodies of water like the Great Lakes. Cities like Istanbul developed at natural crossroads where land met land (in this case, Europe meets Asia) via water. Hence, so many powerful cities in history are closely linked to a body of water, like London on the Thames and Baghdad on the Tigris. European settlement in the New World followed the major rivers, and city concentrations can still be seen on maps up the Hudson and down the Mississippi Rivers and clustered along the shores of the Great Lakes. Interestingly, the largest river in the world, the Amazon in South America, has no bridges that cross it at any point. Not surprisingly, settlements along its banks remain relatively small.

In American settlement, the Great Lakes became the watery highways to port cities that sprung up, including Detroit and Chicago. Families moved in along the waterways, particularly the major rivers, followed later by trains and cars. Eight future United States presidents (nearly a fifth of our presidents) were born on the shores of the Ohio River because their families were migrating and settling along its banks.

Water can also be threatening to humans, as the 2016 floods in Eastern North Carolina following Hurricane Matthew demonstrated. Ironically, the floods were made worse by human development like concrete parking lots and paved roads that prevented the soil in that location from absorbing excess water. Large cities like New Orleans and Phoenix have in modern times demonstrated the challenges of living in places not considered habitable for water reasons. Too much water or too little water can be equally challenging.

The local North Carolina colonial settlement of Salem by the Moravians in the 1760s tells an interesting water story. The church group had purchased nearly 100,000 acres so had ample room to pick a flat place to build their town of Salem but instead chose a hill because natural springs at the top provided water. From this natural water source near present-day Spring Street in Winston-Salem, they used the force of gravity and hollowed out logs to direct the water down the hill to several outdoor water pumps and even indoor faucets, most of which still function today. The original logs are often still being discovered in local digs. This type of community water supply was unheard of in the eighteenth century and even was a point of interest that brought President George Washington to visit the town in 1791 to study the water system and get ideas for his home, Mount Vernon.

Land is also where the water and the air and the soil nourished life as children grew up, calling that place home. Young boys and girls played with the land resources by making sandcastles or rock towns or toys from lumber

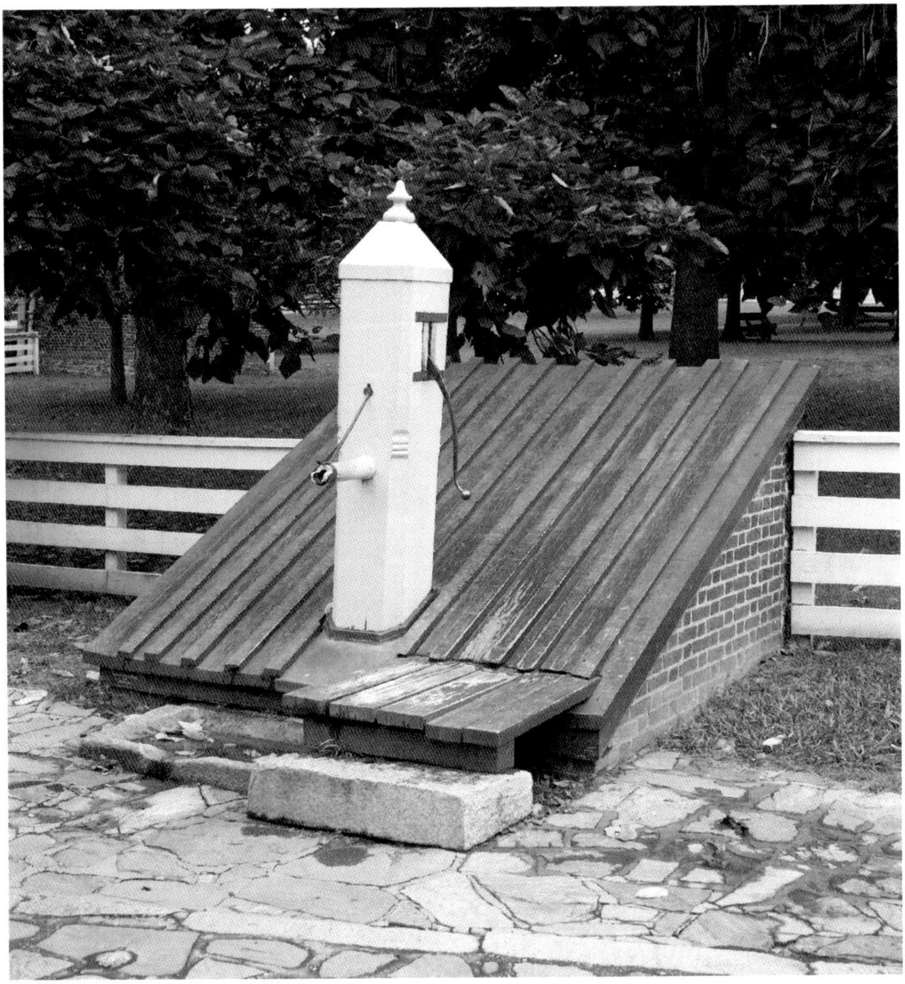

Water pump at Old Salem that was part of the eighteenth-century water system in the town of Salem. *Collection of the author.*

scraps. They wrote with quill pens from goose feathers and molded clay into dolls and marbles. They made pets of local wildlife and floated boats made from tree bark down creeks toward the great beyond. More than bodies were being nourished; skills, imagination and dreams were being fed.

These playing children grew up to follow those dreams, sometimes at that location, and sometimes the dreams took them elsewhere. Dreams accomplished in the centuries of United States history often reflected adventure, exploration of the unknown or mental challenges to find solutions. America is famous worldwide for always seeking to "build a better mousetrap," initially to control a natural problem. What role did the places where the dreams began play in the development of the game changers? Was it the soil itself or the space to dream that produced courage? Was it the challenge to overcome natural obstacles and tame the land that created a pioneer spirit? Was it the environment that built into the human intellect and imagination a desire to do more, to find a way to eliminate limitations and expand horizons? Or did a tougher environment produce a strong back and stronger will? Did the land simply lend itself to the development of skills? Or did the place become part of the person?

In Davie County in the Piedmont area of North Carolina's mountains, like so many other places, land became home to developing minds and bodies and wills. Home is where everyone's story begins, and for three young men, it began on a remote piece of earth with all the ingredients for their future lives.

A hunter tiptoed quietly through the woods, a young man fished on the bank of a creek, a boy thrust a paper airplane into the sky—and dreams were born. Later, these little-known residents left for the larger world and became game changers in history. It is easy to assume that history most often happens in important places such as New York City and Washington, D.C., but that is a mistake. History also happens in smaller, less obvious places like a rural countryside where no one is watching.

This is the story of how rural Davie County in North Carolina provided the rich setting for heroes to grow up in and then gave three of its native sons to the nation: Daniel Boone, Hinton Helper and Thomas Ferebee.

*Chapter 2*

# A Good Piece of Land

Today, as U.S. Highway 64 leaves the town of Mocksville and winds its way westward toward Statesville, it twists past rolling hills and classic southern farms. Fences separate cows from cars and grass from graded asphalt and trees from telephone poles. It is as if two very different eras have begrudgingly agreed to share the same space. Nature has been subdued by machinery and made more livable in the process. Progress has left its footprints on raw land and, in so doing, has tamed the natural world into living places and gardens. Men have trodden down the path that became a wagon road and then later a paved highway. What they first found here was good soil and peaceful woods, not without its dangers. What they have left behind is control over chaos but also sometimes increased noise and risk. Remarkably though, when looking from the highway toward the farmland, it looks more like the same place as centuries ago than less like it. Nature has managed to hold its own even while being invaded by the modern world.

U.S. Highway 64 was given its name in 1926 when the American Association of State Highway Officials connected primary roads in various states to make nation-spanning travel routes with a uniform designation. So the previous local road became part of a federal highway that connects the Outer Banks of North Carolina with a continuous ribbon of 2,326 miles of asphalt that shoots west as far as just shy of the Four Corners, where the states of Arizona, New Mexico, Colorado and Utah meet. U.S. Highway 64 spans three-quarters of the North American continent from east to west. It is the longest road in the

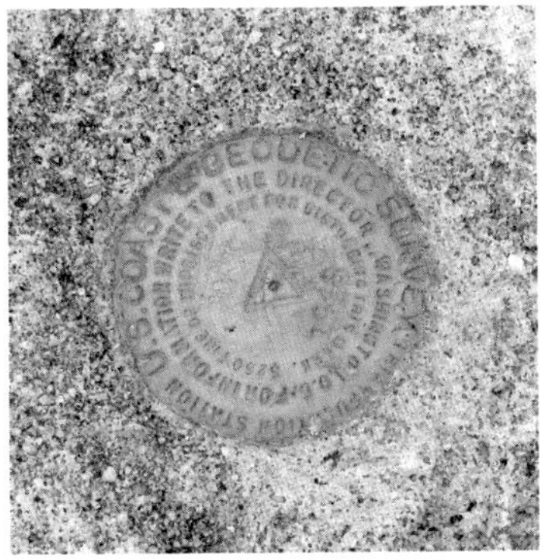

*Right*: United States Geological Society marker in the cemetery of Fork Baptist Church. *Collection of the author.*

*Below*: U.S. Highway 64 winds westward out of Davie County toward higher land. *Collection of the author.*

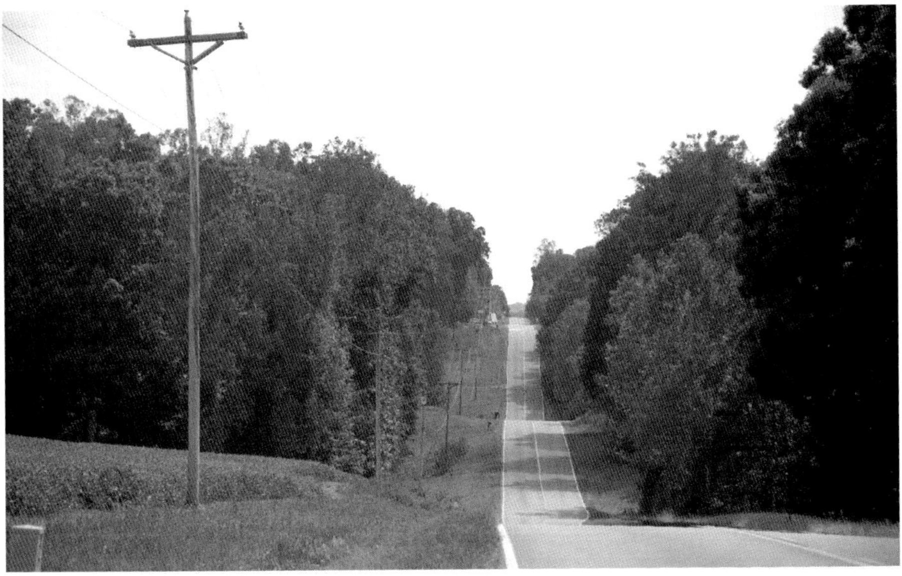

state of North Carolina and links the easternmost town of Manteo with the western edge town of Murphy 604 miles later, slightly reflecting the number assigned to it. One-fourth of this great national road that links the East Coast to the West runs across the wide state of North Carolina.

The land cooperates with man here in Davie County. The Blue Ridge Mountains, part of the Appalachian Mountain Range to the west, gradually descend into flatter land in this area, called the Piedmont (which comes from Latin for "foot of the mountains," or more commonly just called the foothills). It is as if a large bound green carpet has become unrolled and cascaded into a bumpy pile before spreading out flat. The hills here were not as high or as difficult to cross for the early pioneers in this more gentle terrain.

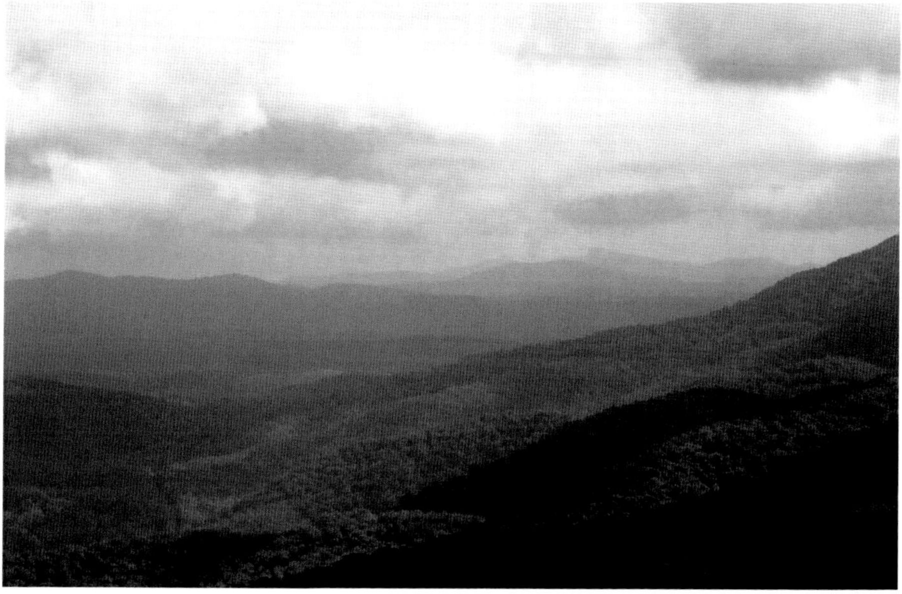

The Blue Ridge Mountains dominate the western topography and views. *Collection of Stephen Phillips.*

One lone mountain protrudes so high in contrast to the flatlands around it that it earned the name Pilot Mountain because it was a navigational point of reference for the surrounding area.

Interestingly, the highest point of elevation, at 1,010 feet, in Davie County is alongside U.S. Highway 64 five miles farther southeast of the farmland in these stories, directly behind historic Fork Baptist Church in a small old community of the same name. A plaque from the United States Geological Society marks the exact spot in the church cemetery.

Even the weather moderates after it crosses the higher elevations in the mountains. It is warmer, less snowy and without the dense mists that give the Smoky Mountains their name. The Piedmont does not feel the effects of the most dangerous climactic conditions. Winters are mild and hot days of summer tolerable, especially on the porches built on homes to catch a breeze while sipping a cold drink. Hurricane rains make it this far inland but are not as destructive generally. Droughts are relatively short-lived. Tornadoes, like the 2017 one that hit Four Corners in Davie County, are rare. Earthquakes are even more so. Surviving weather extremes is not a foremost challenge here. This location and topography, well watered and with rich soil, is ideal for human habitation.

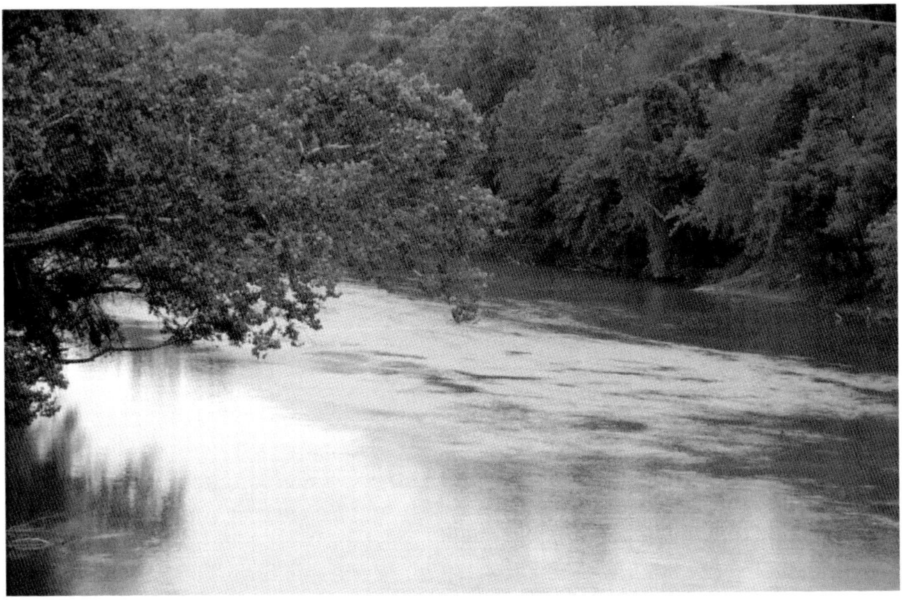

The Yadkin River, in whose forks lies Davie County. *Collection of the author.*

Early settlers found the foothills a perfect place to relocate, not as rugged or forbidding as the mountains but still isolated enough to allow them to be independent. Many of the earliest white settlers in the Piedmont were of Scots-Irish descent, known to be fiercely independent, and they were farmers. The land provided good fertile soil of loam, a type of soil that consists of sand, silt and lesser amounts of clay.

Red clay can be an obstacle to planting but is ideal for pottery, which was then a necessary part of everyday life. Clay used to make pottery is more than just dirt and water or mud. It is enhanced mud because it contains minerals that are usually found in a sedentary location like a creek bed where water deposits the minerals. Minerals mostly required are silica and oxides that are easily broken down by constant underwater forces and abrasion. The clay historically would have to be processed to be usable, but finding good natural clay was the most important starting point. Potters often had favorite locations in local rivers and creeks to find the best clay and set up their kilns nearby.

The land was well watered by rivers and creeks. The Piedmont of North Carolina has an abundance of such waterways. The nearby Yadkin River begins as a creek near Blowing Rock (just east of the Eastern Continental

Divide) and courses its way along 215 miles, making it one of the longest rivers in the state, to the ocean in another state, South Carolina. The Eastern Continental Divide in the Appalachian Mountain Range and the Western Continental Divide in the Rocky Mountains mark the highest points of elevation from where the rivers then have to flow in opposite directions. From the Eastern Continental Divide, rivers flow east to the Atlantic Ocean or west to the Mississippi River. Strictly speaking, the Eastern Continental Divide is not a continental divide in the truest form, since the rivers coursing westward toward the Mississippi River empty water into the Gulf of Mexico, which feeds the Atlantic Ocean, but it approaches it from a different direction at the highest point in the mountains. From the Western Continental Divide, rivers flow west to the Pacific Ocean or east to the Mississippi River, respectively. Water can do many things, but it does not naturally flow uphill.

Rivers provide many things besides water—fish, clay, a power source, a transportation route and an obstruction to travel. Early wayfarers could travel down a river but also looked for shallow places to cross, called fords. The most famous locally is Shallowford on the Yadkin River. A good crossing place required not just shallow water but also accessible banks on both sides. Footmen and horses and then wagons and finally early automobiles (ironically, many of these crossing the ford had the name Ford on them, thanks to Henry Ford, whose development of the assembly line and affordable cars changed the landscape of roads in the twentieth century) followed maps for such a good crossing place before bridges lifted everyone high above rushing water. Crossing a river of moving water was often dangerous and even became a metaphor for death. Flowing water was also harnessed as a power source for mills, both sawmills for lumber and gristmills for grain, before electric power was available. Larger early settlements had mills nearby, and most were powered by water.

Rivers also served as landmarks by which locations were identified. Davie County was identified as being in the Forks of the Yadkin River, and small waterways, tributaries and creeks would be identified as being the river basin of the larger river. One such creek has long been called Bear Creek. No one knows for sure the source of the name, but it is easy to speculate. Legend holds that Daniel Boone and his father gave the creek its name due to the great number of bears trapped there, supposedly ninety-nine in one season. (Interestingly, the bear population that receded with the increase of populated towns has again emerged as the bears' natural habitat space shrunk.)

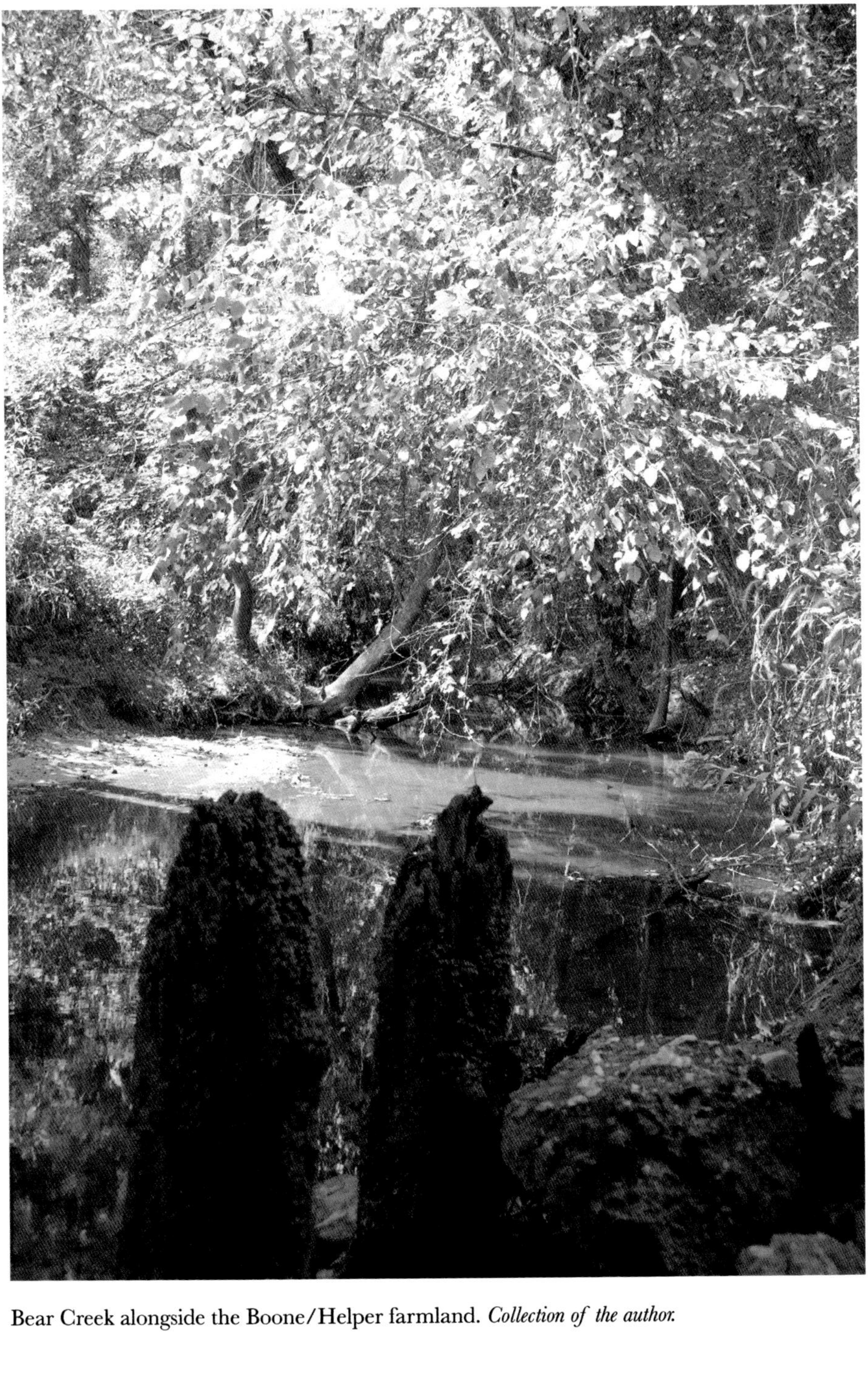

Bear Creek alongside the Boone/Helper farmland. *Collection of the author.*

Sometimes when written historical record is slim as to the origins of a name, a history detective must use common sense but realize it is still speculation, a guess based on some reasonable supposition. Place names often tell their own stories and are intriguing to investigate. Other waterways in North Carolina were given the names Panther Creek and Alligator River, making Bear Creek sound like a tame choice. The New River on the North Carolina/Virginia border was given its name by Peter Jefferson, a surveyor and one of the few white men to explore the area before Daniel Boone would some twenty years later. Daniel was only fifteen at that time and still migrating south from Pennsylvania with his family; Peter Jefferson's six-year-old son Thomas was playing at home, decades away from writing the Declaration of Independence and being the third president of a country that did not yet exist.

North Carolina is unique along the Eastern Seaboard of the United States in that it does not have a major river that flows west to east or that ships can travel very far inland. It has only one that pours out into the ocean, the Cape Fear River (the name suggests how it was perceived originally, but the word "Cape" also indicates its usefulness as a port). Many other lesser rivers empty into it, and it empties into the Atlantic Ocean between Southport and Oak Island. The Cape Fear River was made navigable only as far inland as Fayetteville, leaving most of the state unreachable by large ships. Traded goods had to be loaded onto wagons and hauled inland from the last dock for centuries. Incidentally, other rivers flow to the coast, but the Outer Banks, that chain of islands strung out like a broken strand of pearls, blocks seagoing vessels. The islands of the Outer Banks are called barrier islands because they are obstacles difficult to overcome, but they provide North Carolinians with popular vacation beaches. A couple of visitors from Ohio named Orville and Wilbur Wright found the sand dunes an excellent place for a soft landing of their trial airplane in 1903, making that the place where aviation history first happened. Both the obstacle of the islands of the Outer Banks and its wide expanse of sand demonstrate how geography can strongly influence history.

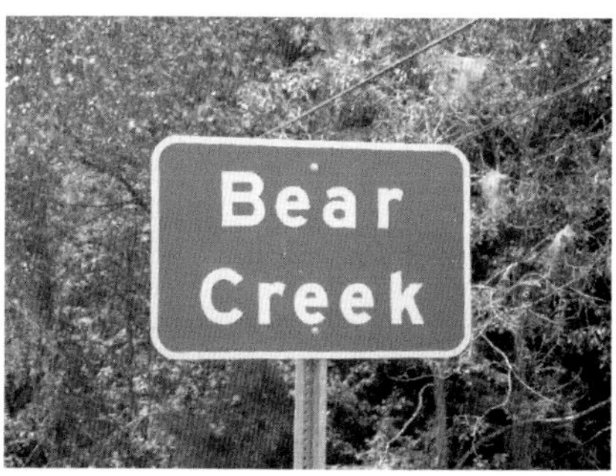


U.S. Highway 64 crosses Bear Creek. *Collection of the author.*

The path that settlers made where Highway 64 now curves its way did not follow Bear Creek but crossed it, perhaps as a shallow ford where it was easier to cross with a wagon. A bridge does the job today, allowing motorists to continue on their journey with only a passing notice of a creek below them. The creek was also a source of water, so essential long before there were pipes underground or faucets in houses. Humans as well as animals accessed the creek water to meet their needs. Often, people came there together or met by random accident at the water's edge. But man and animal also collided there as boys caught fish or hunted bear. Another nearby creek in Davie County called Hunting Creek clearly indicates what happened there.

The land in northwestern North Carolina has long been called the backcountry because it lies behind or in back of the fall line. This imaginary line that geographically runs near Raleigh marks the point where the land

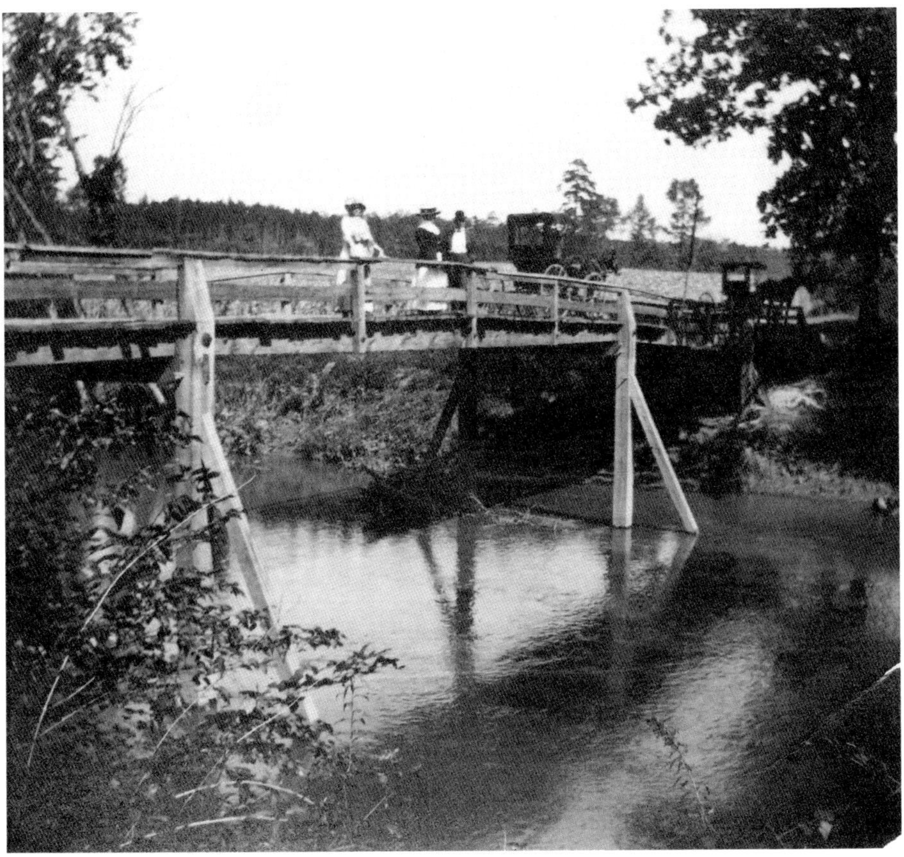

Early twentieth-century photograph of residents enjoying Hunting Creek. *Collection of Davie County Public Library.*

flattens out and the rivers, therefore, fan out toward the eastern coast. The people of the backcountry were by no means backwards, but that might have been the impression of those living farther east.

The backcountry in the colonial era also was known as the place where settlers fought the more established communities in the East over almost everything, but specifically over taxation in the War of the Regulation of the 1760–70s (but that is another story). It may seem strange that while fighting the British and the French and the Indians, fellow colonists and pioneers also often fought each other in North Carolina in the 1700s. They had less in common than one would imagine. The Eastern North Carolina settlers had come directly from England and continued to hug the coastal region and look back toward the Old World while the western part of the state was settled by Scots-Irish, Germans and others who came down the Great Wagon Road from northern colonies, mostly Pennsylvania. They were fiercely independent (particularly due to their history in dealings with the British in the Old World) and without powerful connections, which they resented. So the notion that settlement gradually spread westward from the coast is a mistaken idea best illustrated by the vast, still unpopulated wooded areas within one hundred miles of the coast. Settlement patterns followed other routes and rarely moved directly west. Vast differences divided the settlers in the east and west of the colony of North Carolina.

The land in the Piedmont was so good that other explorers commented on it. William Byrd was an important Virginian, credited with founding the city of Richmond (later to be the capital of the Confederacy) and with being an early advocate of the smallpox inoculation after his wife died from the disease. He also helped settle the border between his state of Virginia and North Carolina and, during those pursuits, explored this area soon to be overrun with settlers. Byrd wrote in 1728 in *Histories of the Dividing Line Betwixt Virginia and North Carolina*: "The Soil is exceedingly rich on both sides of the Yadkin, abounding in rank grass and prodigiously large trees; and for plenty of Fish, Fowel [*sic*] and Venison is inferior to No Part of the Northern Continent." He also wrote to fellow explorer Mark Catesby of "green canes," probably reeds and bamboo that were sixteen feet high and provided forage for buffalo. It is hard to imagine buffalo in central North Carolina, but the space and plant life present then could have supported buffalo herds, and the sightings of buffalo tracks were further proof that they made this region their home before humans did.

Another explorer of the area that later became Davie County, John Lawson, wrote in his book titled *A New Voyage to Carolina* of the combination

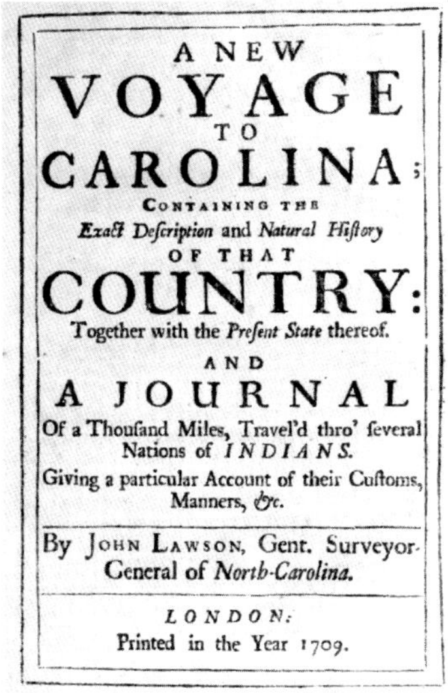

A NEW
VOYAGE
TO
CAROLINA;
Containing the
*Exact Deſcription* and *Natural Hiſtory*
OF THAT
COUNTRY:
Together with the *Preſent State* thereof.
AND
A JOURNAL
Of a Thouſand Miles, Travel'd thro' ſeveral Nations of *INDIANS*.
Giving a particular Account of their Cuſtoms, Manners, *&c.*

By John Lawson, Gent. Surveyor-General of *North-Carolina*.

*LONDON:*
Printed in the Year 1709.

John Lawson's 1701 book *A New Voyage to Carolina* described the circa 1700 Piedmont prior to English settlement. *Collection of Wilson Special Collection Library, UNC–Chapel Hill.*

of forests of hardwoods like oak, pine, hickory and poplar with stones readily available for building structures or walls alongside areas that were large clearings, almost like savannas (a term most associated with African grasslands). Davie County historian James Wall of Mocksville would later surmise that many of these clearings were the result of Native American activity, such as burning off the forest to push deer into the opening to hunt. He believed the community of Farmington in Davie County was such a case. Regardless of whether the clearings were natural or man-made, this was an almost ideal combination of the rocks needed for foundations, trees needed to build and open land for planting.

The earliest European settlements in the New World were first and foremost around forts, built to defend a claim to land and the people settling there. Forts are best situated on very particular land. While there must be rocks or timber available locally to use as building materials, the location and foundation determined the building site. So those in charge who first climbed off the boats in the earliest colonies of St. Augustine, Quebec, Virginia and Massachusetts made it their foremost priority to determine a site for a fort. It needed a strategic location to spot enemy attacks, which usually meant a clearing on the highest land around. The fort also needed to be built on solid ground, hopefully solid rock that could not be undermined by weather, water or enemies. But by the time the first settlers were filtering into Western North Carolina a century later, fortresses like Fort Dobbs and the one at Tanglewood were becoming less common than trading posts and taverns. The risk of attack was still present and would influence their building of structures like a wooden defensive fence at Bethabara, the neighboring first Moravian settlement, but soon fences more often encircled gardens to keep out the risk of animals, not humans.

That trees were abundant in the Piedmont is evidenced in the name given by the Sioux people to the Yadkin River. The word Yadkin means "big trees" in their language, which might have been a reference to the size of the trees but also possibly to their number. Either way, wood from trees was plentiful. A wide range of types of trees grew naturally in the area, including poplar, sycamore, maple (which supplied syrup), hickory (for which a North Carolina city is named today) and oak, long considered ideal for many building purposes due to its flexibility and strength. Other trees provided wood for burning fires, necessary for warmth, cooking and light.

One firsthand contemporary account of the area was given by a Moravian by the name of Bishop August Gottlieb Spangenberg. In his journal, he wrote of the tall trees, green reeds and buffalo tracks, as well as the presence of many creeks. He mentions by name the Chinquapin trees, for which a small community in northern Davie County is named. Bishop Spangenberg was a German minister of a Protestant church, called Moravians by others due to their European point of origin, that had relocated from Europe to Pennsylvania. In November 1752, Spangenberg was with a group scouting out a location for a new community in North Carolina they would call Salem. It was the first settlement that would later become the present-day city of Winston-Salem.

Moravian accounts in 1760 also mention the abundance of wildlife, including wolves, panthers, wild turkeys and bear, including one of the latter that reportedly weighed three hundred pounds. Even the rare buffalo was still being seen. Buffalo (technically the species of animals known as bison) is today the official American mammal. As late as 1750,

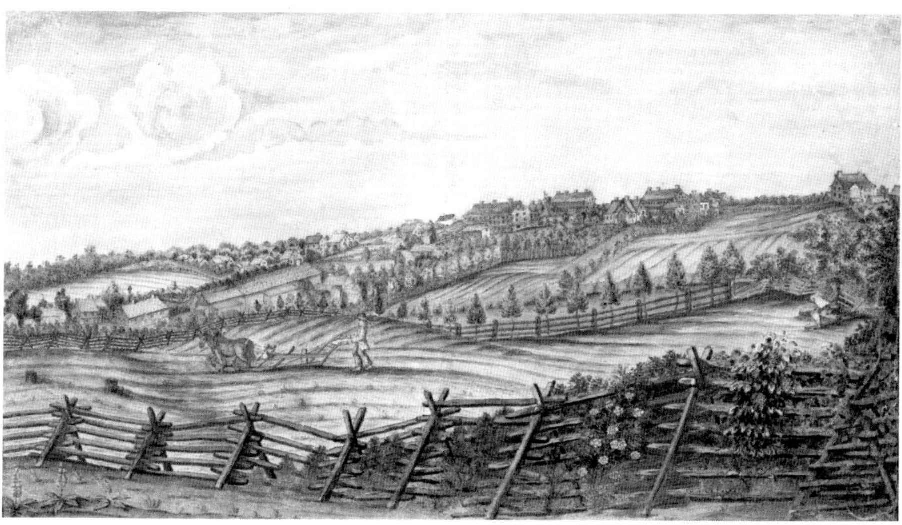

A 1787 painting of the town of Salem by Ludwig von Redeken. *Collection of Museum of Early Southern Decorative Arts, Old Salem Museums and Gardens.*

there was a documented sighting of buffalo at the Catawba River just west of Davie County. Buffalo were so vastly hunted by Indians, Europeans and settlers that they nearly went extinct. In 1900, there were only about 300 buffalo known to be living in the United States, but diligent efforts to protect them resulted in there being 360,000 known alive in 2000, a miraculous animal rescue.

Wild animals were drawn to salt licks, natural deposits of salt concentrations commonly found on Dutchman Creek, another tributary of the Yadkin River in Davie County. One such salt lick was reported to be two to three feet deep and as much as six feet wide. These were important because hunters could count on finding animals at salt licks. Most food today has plenty of salt already processed in it, but throughout much of history, it was a dietary need for animals and humans that was often in small supply except in the salt water of the oceans. Interestingly, people need fresh water to drink but also need the salt from the water they cannot drink. For centuries, salt had to be condensed from a water source and sold at a high price. So valuable was it that Roman soldiers were paid in salt; hence, the modern English word "salary" comes from the Latin word for salt.

Along with the deer, bear and turkeys, settlers found plentiful pigeons that had served as a main food source for the native Indians and the white hunters. Birds often flocked to rivers and creeks because they also "fished" for dinner, but that meant they were easily picked off for human consumption there as well. Observers also noted the presence of another wild animal in large numbers—snakes—and there were records of multiple snakebites from poisonous snakes resulting in deaths.

Catfish, bass and trout filled the streams that were frequently described as "silvery" from their presence. Native Americans had built V-shaped rock dams to trap the fish, and there are archaeological remains of camps along the riverside that reveal this was a regular food harvest for them. There were several branches of the Sioux tribe, as well as Catawba and Cherokee Indians in the area. The Sioux were the fiercest, and it is possible the famous explorer John Lawson was tortured and killed by them. The Indians first felt threatened as competition for the hunting grounds increased. The Catawba tribe was friendlier than others, but that cost them, as they were exposed to smallpox, a disease of the white men for which they had no natural immunity, and were nearly wiped out. Increasingly, Native American people groups became an obstacle to overcome for the white settlers.

The exchange between the native people of the New World and the Europeans who were arriving in waves was many times confrontational, and

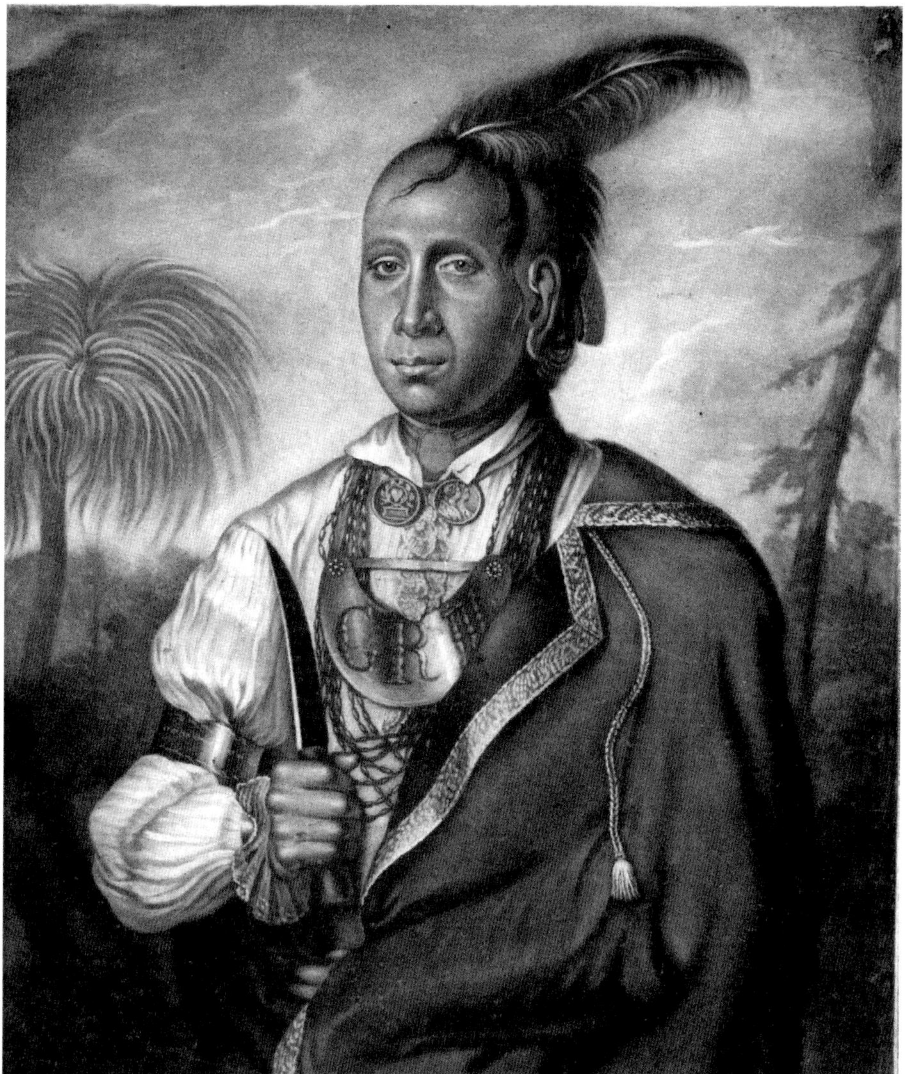

Cherokee chief Cunne Shote in a James McArdell engraving from a 1762 London painting by Francis Parsons. *Collection of Museum of Early Southern Decorative Arts, Old Salem Museums and Gardens.*

fighting ensued. But there were also cultural exchanges as they learned from each other. Indians were often taken to the Old World as a curiosity, no doubt a shared sentiment. New foods like corn and tomatoes were introduced and taken back to the far shores across the ocean. Pumpkins native to North America held less appeal to the white settlers, but several towns survived tough winters and the threat of starvation by eating mostly pumpkin. Technology like metal working from the Old World made life easier in the new. But Native Americans quickly learned that arrows were no match for gunfire. Increasingly, the natives were outnumbered. They were migratory and did not have the same concept of landownership as Europeans. Old-world diseases inflicted unprotected tribes. They were vulnerable and suffered accordingly. Mostly, the results of this cultural exchange did not favor the original inhabitants.

The interaction between the Native Americans and the white settlers most often began in a trading relationship from which both parties benefited. This was true across North America, where often furs were traded for European muskets, but arming the other party quickly proved to be a mistake when the relationship went bad. One local legend tells of the severed head of a white scout being held up toward the eastern sun to warn the whites of the result of their encroachment. Moravian records from 1759 tell of some members being killed along the Yadkin River by the natives and the refugees retreating to Bethabara. A fort was built for protection in the present-day Tanglewood Park on the Yadkin River, which serves now as the boundary between Davie and Forsyth Counties. But initially, most trades were friendly. A trading path from Fort Dobbs, built to defend the settlers from the Indians who were allied with the French in the aptly named French and Indian War, continued down into the area to Trading Ford on the Yadkin River, a location name that tells its reason for existence. Some of the first settlements, not surprisingly, were trading posts where the two parties met at a good central location.

Colonial roads were far different than the ones traveled today. They were not planned as later developments in the Midwest, where roads still reflect the grid pattern of the Northwest Ordinance. The Northwest Land Ordinance and the Land Ordinance of 1785 laid out land lots in the Midwest as one-mile squares in a township. As lots were sold and settled, the roads followed the lines of the division to avoid crossing private property and therefore created a grid pattern, still visible from the air and in road names such as Five Mile Road.

Where Native American people had created a footpath through woods along the easiest grade, explorers and traders forged through, and then settlers and wagons followed. Nothing was by plan or deliberate; people repeatedly followed the open path and rarely cut across the shortest distance. Roads curved when it was easier to go around than move a boulder or cut down a large tree, and the curves may still show up in the road today with no visible reason why. The old term "palimpsest" referred to ancient manuscripts of

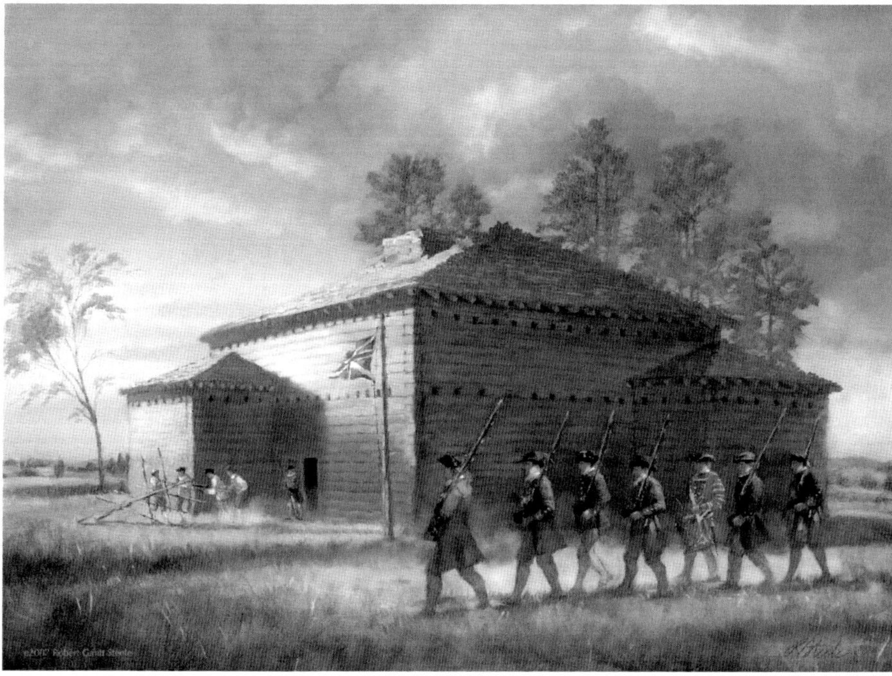

Painting of colonial Fort Dobbs, built for protection of settlers from Indians. *Collection of Fort Dobbs.*

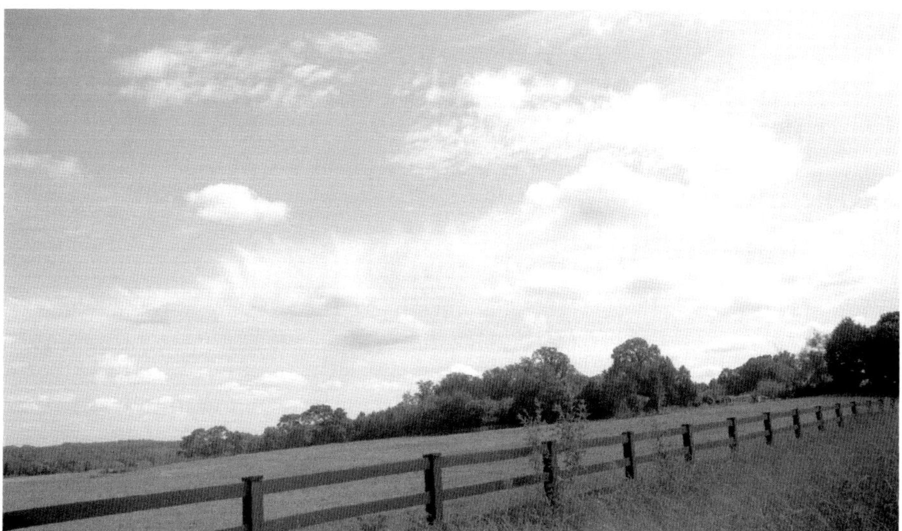

The Piedmont's rolling, fertile farmland. *Collection of Stephen Phillips.*

parchment that could be cleaned and reused, yet often left the previous message still visible. Now the term can refer to any faint indication of a previous item, rather like a disappearing message from the past. The curve in the road where the boulder or tree is now gone is a palimpsest.

Unlike present paved roads, the roads then were rough, to greatly understate the condition. They were mostly just hardened dirt but full of rocks and ruts where nothing prevented water from draining in the path of least resistance, as water does. After heavy rains and snow melts, roads were so muddy that they were impassable for wheels, animals or even men to travel. There is a legendary story of a man taking produce to a market in colonial times who found his progress so slow at the end of the first day that he set down his goods and returned home to spend the night before continuing. But the fearless early settlers in North Carolina had no alternative, and their determination pushed them forward. Those who survived passed on that stubborn determination to their descendants.

Settlers coming into the Piedmont area of North Carolina encountered many obstacles, but the pull of well-watered fertile soil and a moderate climate attracted them more than the problems deterred them. After all, in the mid-1700s, new lands everywhere came with struggles. This one did also but gave in return great views and the potential for a good life. It was considered a fair enough tradeoff to people who lived in a barter culture. Barter was the most common form of exchange when money was scarce. It consisted of exchanging a product or service for another, based on similar value. Due to the history of colonization in colonial America, various currencies (Spanish, English and those of the individual colonies) circulated, and it was difficult to figure out the exchange rate between them. Merchants had no choice but to do the math, but the average person found it easier to simply trade what he had for what he needed. So the first settlers in this region were willing to trade hard labor and determination for a chance to live on this beautiful land.

The land in the Piedmont that would later become Davie County was prime real estate and ready for settlement when the adventurous first settlers arrived in the mid-1700s. The Boone family was among them.

*Chapter 3*

# DANIEL BOONE

Daniel Boone was just a small child living in Pennsylvania when the first white settlers came into the area that is present-day Davie County, west of the Yadkin River, in the 1740s. At that time, it was considered part of Anson County in the British colony of North Carolina, named for a British admiral who circumnavigated the globe but never set foot in North Carolina. Boone, the restless explorer, would more than just set foot in North Carolina; he would come here as a teen in an early wave of migrating settlers and over the next twenty years be molded by the place into the great hunter and pioneer of the West. Among the first white settlers in Davie County was the most famous of its residents.

Sadly, Anson County records were destroyed in a courthouse fire in 1868, so little can be documented from the earliest years. This type of disaster tells the story of the challenge of history. History can only be studied if original records, also called primary sources, survive to tell the story. For instance, Daniel Boone's own handwritten autobiography was lost in 1814 when his canoe overturned and the pages floated down the Missouri River. Many years later, a Wisconsin historian named Lyman Draper spent his life researching Daniel Boone's life and interviewed Boone's last living child, Nathan, as well as receiving hundreds of family notes from him. On his stagecoach ride home, the trunk holding this written treasure-trove bounced off and was lost. According to Ted Franklin Belue, who edited Draper's writing and published his book, Draper spent days searching the area and finally found the trunk in the hands of an honest man, thus saving this cache of primary sources for the historical record. Interestingly, statistics show that fire is the third greatest threat to old documents. Water in any form, such as floods or humidity, is the second. The number one greatest threat to old papers is humans, who destroy, lose, steal or otherwise damage bits and pieces of history. The primary sources regarding Daniel Boone were significantly influenced by all three of these risks.

In 1753, the area near the present-day town of Mocksville became part of a large county called Rowan, named for an Irishman who was a reformed smuggler and briefly governor of the colony of North Carolina, but there is not any clear indication that he ever came to the county named for him either. Rowan County still exists today with Salisbury as its county seat, but the county is much smaller now than it was then. The area of land in this story became part of the newly created Davie County in 1836, when the state gradually was divided into more counties. It was named for William R. Davie, tenth governor of North Carolina, and it seems he must have at least traveled through the area later named for him (as would be the William R. Davie Elementary School on Highway 601). Legend says that North Carolina counties were formed when each had a courthouse, a jailhouse and a warehouse. Mocksville built its first jailhouse one year later in 1837, perhaps to qualify.

Some historians believe Morgan Bryan, one of the first settlers in the area near Bear Creek in 1748, came to this location to operate a trading post, as he had in Virginia. But it was the dirt that kept him here, as he stayed to farm the fertile soil he discovered. Bryan was a Quaker from Pennsylvania and the patriarch of a large family that occupied what became known as Bryan Settlement, sized five thousand acres (approximately eight square miles). His land claim became a landmark referenced by the Moravians and many others. He was seventy-seven when he arrived, so it was left to his descendants to populate the territory. Legend says he was buried in historic Joppa Cemetery, on the outskirts of present-day Mocksville, but there is no proof or physical marker to identify it.

This was a time when many Americans were immigrants from the Old World and seemed to be constantly moving on in the New World as well. Having left any familiar territory, perhaps they did not feel tied to one location. Or perhaps it was just the timeless wanderlust of wanting to see what was beyond the next hill. Maybe they were just restless dreamers whose nomadic lives suited them. Regardless, many family tales from this era speak of multiple relocations until settling in one place that many future generations would call home. The reasons that determine a family's choice

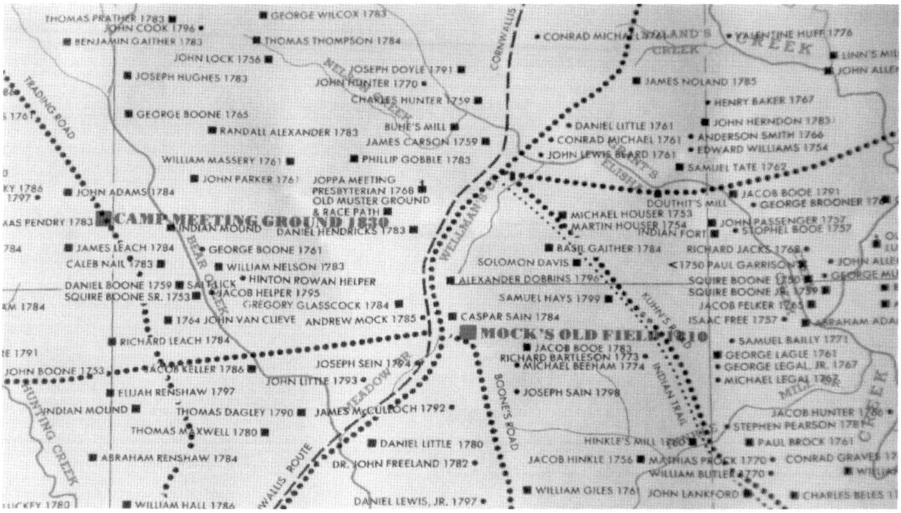


A 1977 Andrew Lagle land grant map of settlers' claims in the mid-1700s in Davie County. *Collection of the author.*

of a place to settle can vary greatly. An anecdotal story tells of one such modern family who migrated south from West Virginia looking for work during the Great Depression of the 1930s. When asked why they picked the Piedmont area of North Carolina to stop and settle, the answer was not because they found work first here but because they had a tankful of gas in the car and that is where they simply ran out of gas.

Bryan was followed by thousands of other settlers relocating down the Great Wagon Road, including a man named Squire Boone. ("Squire" was also a medieval title of nobility from the Old World used to designate a knight rewarded with large landholdings, but in this case it was just his name, perhaps bestowed by hopeful parents who dreamed he would become the large landowner he ultimately did.) Squire Boone was born in England in 1696, making him truly a man from another country and another century. He immigrated to Pennsylvania at age seventeen, and his parents followed him across the ocean later. It was a bold and brave leap of faith for a teenager to travel to the unknown. But he was quickly absorbed into a community of Quaker Friends of like faith and soon married fellow Quaker Sarah Morgan. Squire and Sarah Boone would have eleven children. The sixth one was a son born in a log cabin while they still lived in the British colony of Pennsylvania on October 22 (now November 2), 1734. They named him Daniel.

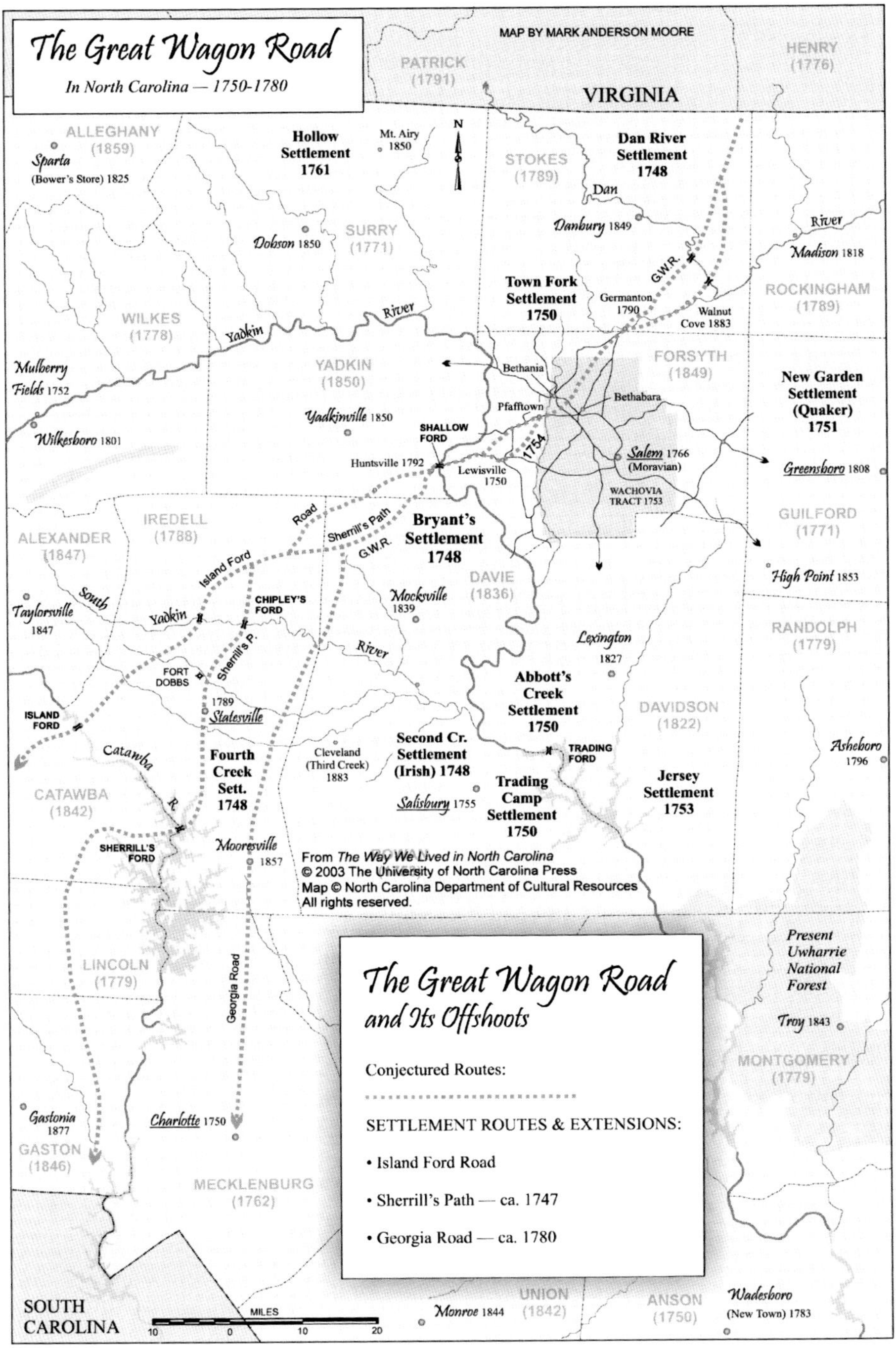


Map of the Great Wagon Road. *Collection of the author.*

Why the difference in dates? The old Julian Calendar, named for Julius Caesar and often referred to as the Old Style, was off just enough to not be aligned correctly with the seasons after centuries of use. The Catholic bishops were concerned that Easter was not being celebrated when it should be, so in 1582 Pope Gregory created an adjustment to the calendar by tweaking how often leap year would be celebrated to bring it back in sync. Initially, the calendar date had to be adjusted to compensate for the lost time. The Gregorian Calendar, sometimes called the New Style calendar, was adopted over the next four centuries (Russia and Greece did not until the twentieth century), by the Catholic countries in Europe first and then, grudgingly, by the Protestants. The switch in colonial America took place during Daniel Boone's lifetime, so he stated his birthdate as October 22, as it was when he was born, but later altered to November 2. Others like George Washington, who was only two years older than Daniel Boone, were affected the same way. Washington's original birthdate was February 11, but Americans celebrate it now on its changed date of February 22. Actually, they now celebrate it as a national holiday on the third Monday in February, so rarely is it celebrated on the changed date and never on Washington's original birthdate.

Squire Boone would migrate yet again with his family, prompted by the dual motives of religious disagreement and the promise of cheap land. This is often called the push/pull factor in settlement geography, where one scenario pushed people out of a place while another reason drew or pulled them to the next location. Sometimes one reason is much stronger than the other, but the famous example of the displacement of many Jews following World War II and the establishment of Israel as a nation shows equally strong dynamics.

Squire and Sarah Boone met with their Quaker church's disapproval twice when one of their children married someone outside his faith. When their son Jonathan married Mary, who was the daughter of James Carter, the founder of the town of Salisbury in the North Carolina colony, the crisis with their church prompting them to leave and the knowledge of cheap land drawing them south merged in a marriage of motivation.

Their trek took a new generation of settlers down the Great Wagon Road, which ran north and south 435 miles, connecting Pennsylvania and the Carolinas. Ultimately, this most traveled road in the colonial era before the American Revolutionary War covered 700 miles between Philadelphia and southern Georgia. The traffic was mostly going one direction—south. Beginning as a footpath in a naturally flat clearing, it

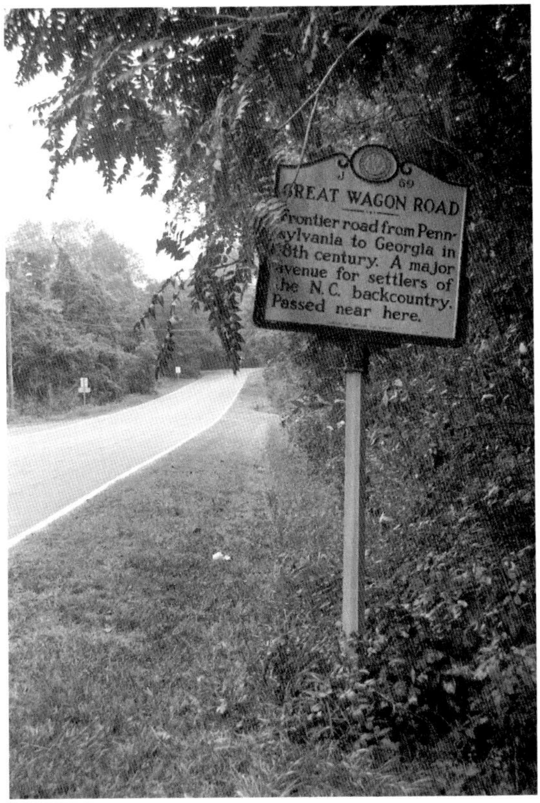


*Right*: Great Wagon Road marker near Bethania on NC 65 in Forsyth County. *Collection of the author.*

*Below*: Yadkin River at Shallowford where the Great Wagon Road headed for Davie County. *Collection of the author.*

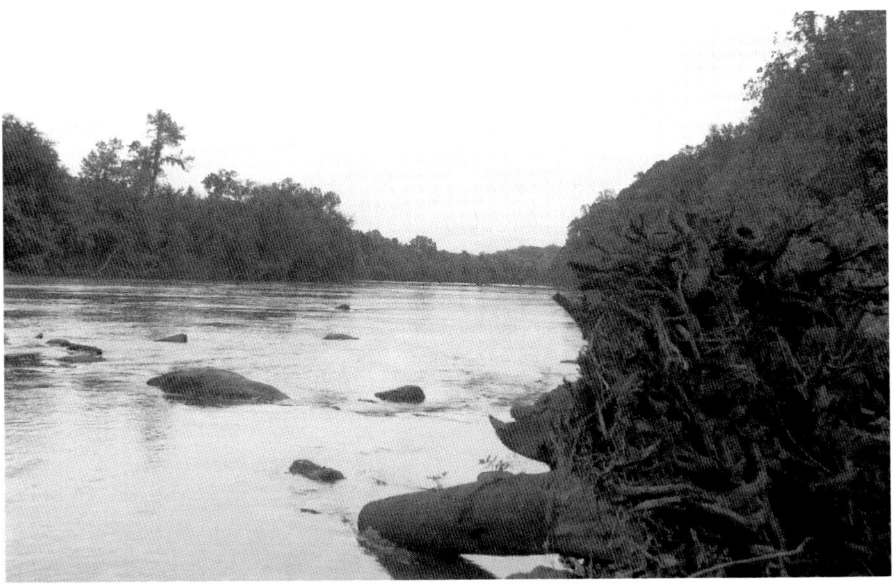

was worn down by the weight of thousands of wagons each year until it became a hardened road bed. Parts of that path are now buried under paved roads or lay slightly off the paved road as newer road-making techniques made it easier to straighten out curves. Having been either a natural hard bed or packed down or both, these stretches of old road often do not make the best farmland and therefore leave traces as the undergrowth reclaims the land.

The Great Wagon Road crossed at Shallowford (on the Yadkin River bordering present-day Yadkin and Forsyth Counties near Lewisville) on its way to Salisbury, a town that began with a land grant from Lord Granville along a historic Indian trading path and quickly grew to be the biggest town in Western North Carolina in the colonial era, largely due to its role as a trading stop on the Great Wagon Road. Bits and pieces of the original Great Wagon Road in Davie County are still visible to the eye in their natural form most similar to how the original road would have appeared. Other reminders include Georgia Road paved over the original road, where licenses show an old tavern stood for travelers and its name indicating where many of the travelers' ultimate goal lay.

The Boone family lingered for a short while in the Shenandoah Valley in Virginia on their way south from Pennsylvania. They eventually continued the trek though, and according to local legend, the family lived briefly in a cave on the north fork of the Yadkin River in present-day Davidson County while securing a homeplace; the cave is today known as Boone's Cave and is open to the public. Its location overlooking the Yadkin River is as natural a place as any associated with the Boones. The cave is small and shallow and would have been suitable mostly just for sleeping but gives anyone willing to crawl inside a strong sense of life on the frontier and why even a small log cabin would have been an improvement. The view from the cave was of the river and the land on the other side, now Davie County.

The Boones eventually settled in the Yadkin River Valley on 640 acres (a square mile of land) in 1753. Squire Boone acquired it from Lord Granville, the British proprietor who still charged a quitrent to the owners, the last vestige of the feudal system that had so long been the way for the powerful to control the poor in Europe. This system was hated and would be an issue in the American Revolutionary War, but it was the initial way land was available to those who could never have owned any before. Landownership had always been the privilege of the upper class in the Old World of Europe. The chance to own one's own land, therefore, was a huge motivation to keep moving.

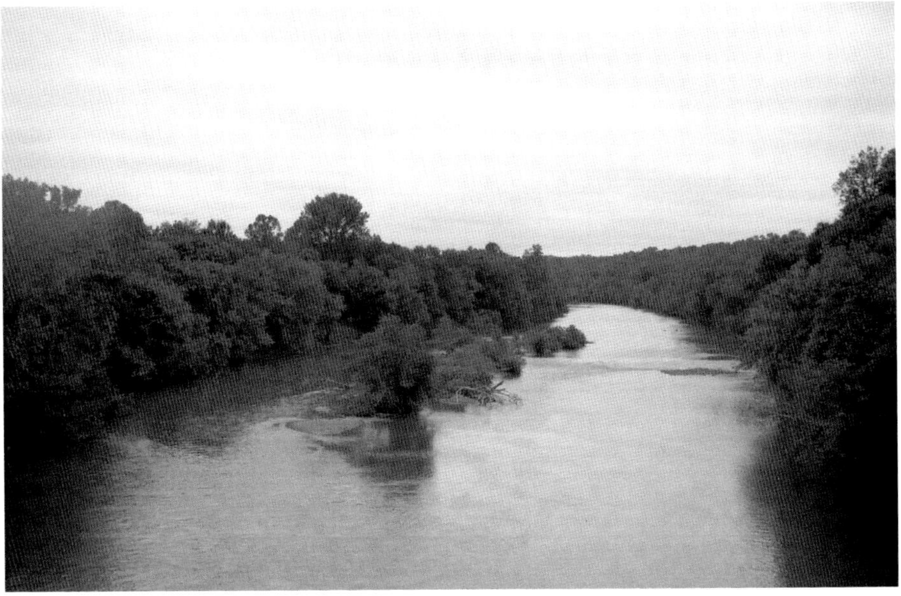

The Squire Boone family first camped along the portion of the Yadkin River that today forms the boundary between Davie and Davidson Counties. *Collection of the author.*

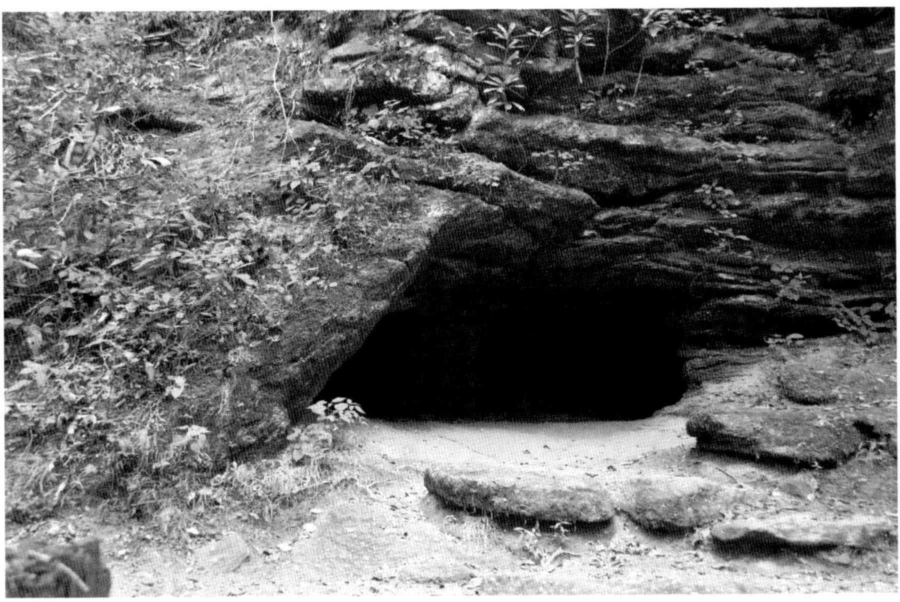

Boone's Cave, where legend says the Boone family first stayed in the area. *Collection of the author.*

One can imagine Squire Boone and his family at their first glimpse of lush green land rolling out before them. They undoubtedly camped out, maybe trying several locations, before deciding where to build a cabin and live. While Squire walked the land and dug up handfuls of dirt to examine, his wife, Sarah, no doubt checked out the distance to the nearest creek bank for hauling water and washing clothes. The kids probably ran rather than walked, excitedly competing with one another to be the first to discover a large tree to climb or a place to hide or other such treasure in play.

Seventeen-year-old Daniel no doubt wandered off by himself, something he was known for his entire life, looking for good hunting and fishing spots. A nice combination made this possible—that he was of an age that he was allowed to wander alone (although getting permission never seemed to matter much to Daniel) and that his dad owned such a large piece of land that he was not actually leaving home…at least not at first. He did not have to go far to find a creek to fish and woods to hunt. Many creeks sliced through the area and were teeming with fish. Furthermore, the animals came there for water, bringing his hunting targets to him. He also loved the challenge of tracking animals and trapping them. The Great Woodsman (as he later was known) would later claim this was the best hunting grounds he ever roamed. It is certainly where he learned and honed his skills. The land became the training ground for this future explorer and hunter. His skills of shooting and making traps improved, and his imagination was fired in frontier wilderness made safe by proximity to home.

Squire Boone quickly acquired a second 640-acre lot in 1753 along the Bear Creek and built a log cabin—only eighteen by twenty-two feet, a sizeable living room in a house today—for his large family. (Some of the logs from this cabin were used in the next century by the Helper family who built there, and part of the original structure stood until 1925.) This was Daniel's home until he married, and afterward, he and his wife and children would live in another cabin on the same farm. Later, he bought this land on Bear Creek from his parents in 1759 (when the older Boones retreated to Virginia for a short while to escape the Indian threat), and deeds show he owned it for the next four years. It appears that he sold it to pay off debts, and the young couple then lived at Sugartree Creek near present-day Farmington for a short while before they moved on.

It is interesting that Daniel Boone's grandfather George Boone and his father, Squire, were weavers by trade, since the word "boon" was the Old English word for the woody fiber from the flax plant that produced linen. Many surnames (last names) came from the craft or trade of the man, such

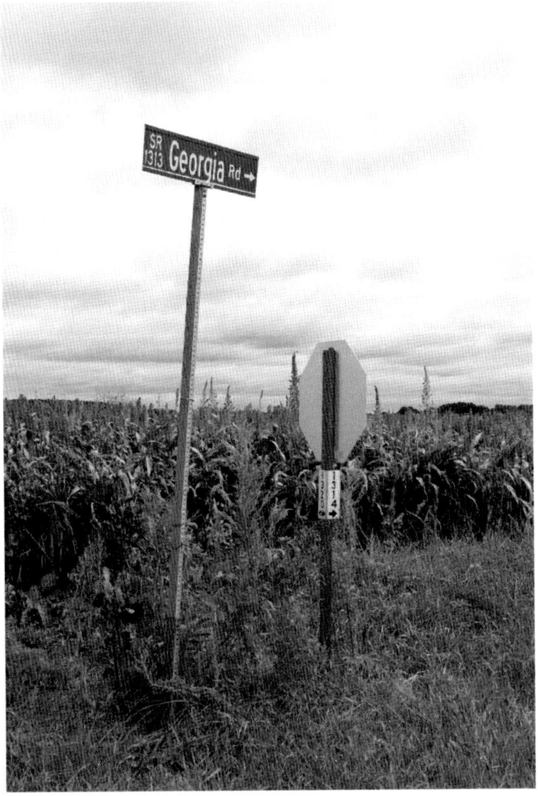


*Left*: Present-day Georgia Road on the path of the Great Wagon Road. *Collection of the author.*

*Below*: Intersection of Bear Creek Church Road and Georgia Road where a tavern once gave travelers rest on their migration south on the Great Wagon Road. *Collection of the author.*

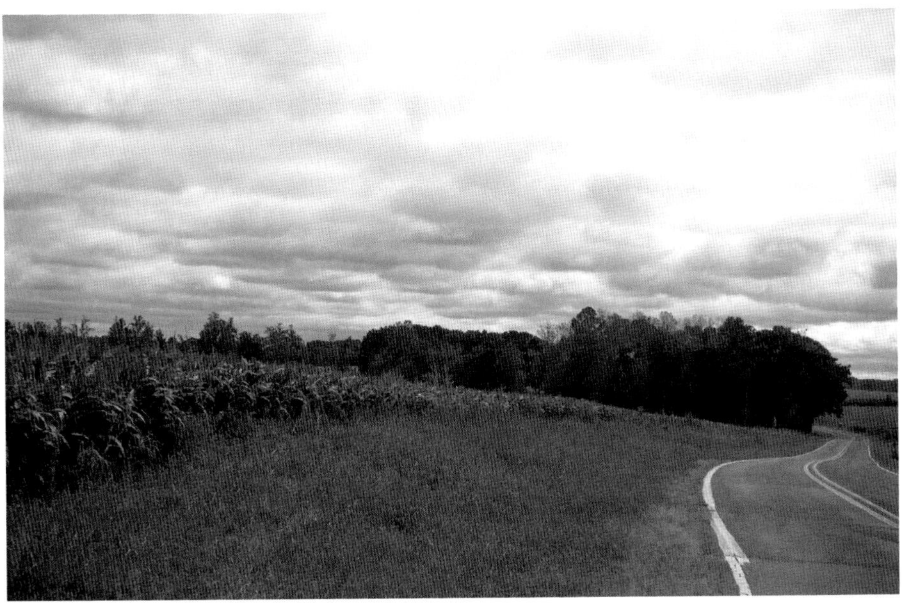

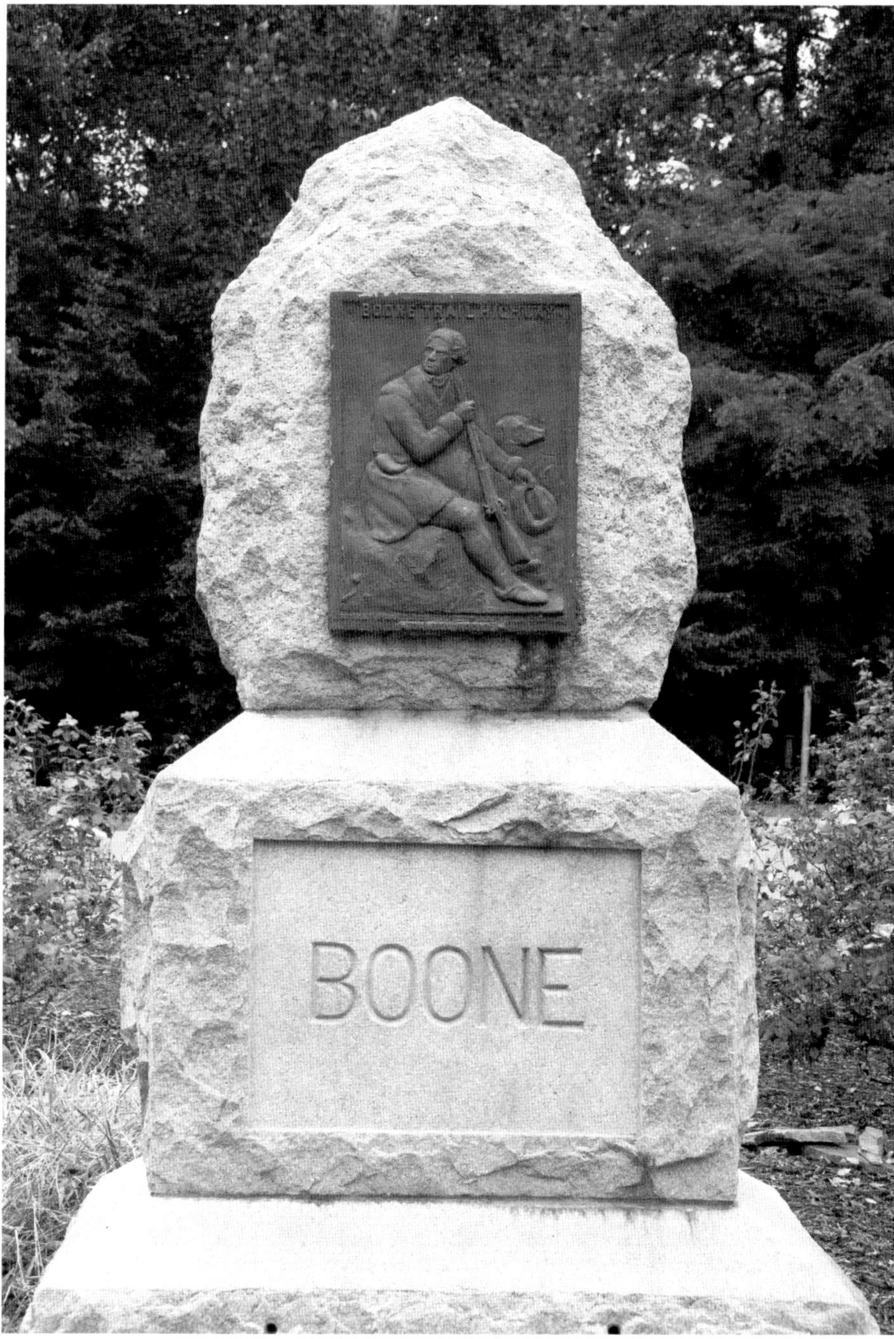


Monument to Daniel Boone at Boone's Cave Park. *Collection of the author.*

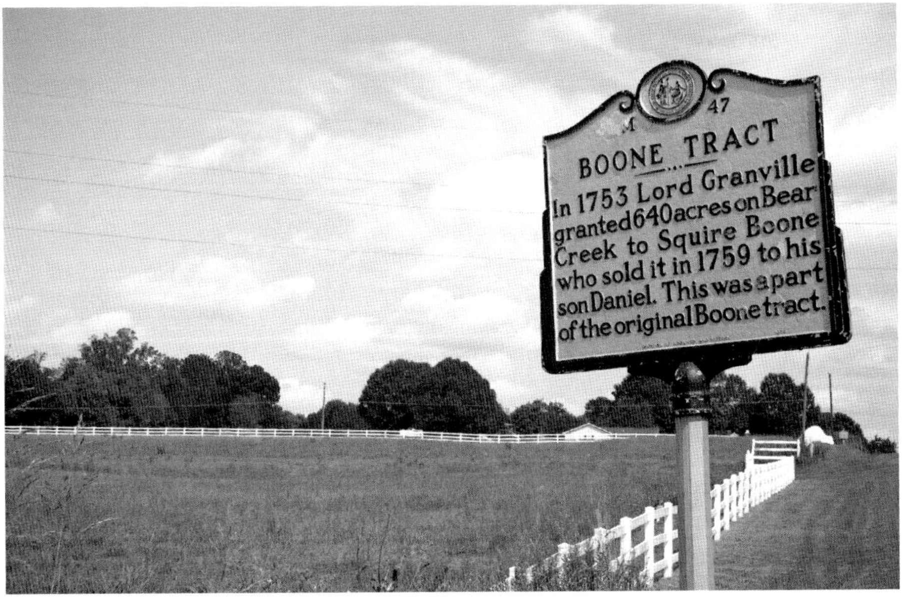


Boone Tract historic sign along U.S. Highway 64 and Bear Creek. *Collection of the author.*

as Cooper (maker of barrels), Carpenter, Baker or Smith (as in gunsmith or blacksmith). Others, of course, reflected family connections such as Johnson. Daniel Boone would reject his ancestors' trade, and had he been the generation to determine the family surname, it would have no doubt been Hunter.

Daniel Boone (who disliked and never wore coonskin caps, contrary to TV legend) favored beaver felt hats and always identified himself as a "woodsman," never as an "Indian fighter." It was in the woods along Bear Creek that he found his first love and his calling in life. Daniel learned to hunt out of necessity, but he also learned how much he loved it, first as a young boy and then as a family man with mouths to feed. He quickly became skilled at making and repairing his own iron traps. He had no access to stores, so he experimented and adapted what he knew to work for him. This ability to innovate would later allow him to hunt in different terrains. He never seemed to be afraid of traveling into unknown and uncharted areas, partly because he always knew he could find a way to hunt and therefore would not starve. He figured all this out on the banks of Bear Creek.

Daniel fit into the wooded terrain as if born for it. He was particularly close to his mother, with whom he shared a love of the outdoors and being alone in it. He camped many summers with her to tend sheep. During these forays, he fell in love with the uncrowded woods and the quiet meadows and turned his back on any other life. The long, deep talks with his mom and the ability to roam the land made him feel at home in the wild.

He was known to go so far afield hunting that he lost track of place and time, as if even as a boy the normal constraints of belonging to a place were rules meant to be broken. Dressed in buckskins and wearing soft leather moccasins, he could sneak up on his prey almost as if camouflaged. He hunted by moonlight and would tell of things he learned from the Indians who no one else ever encountered. This began a lifelong habit for Daniel of forging friendships and learning from the Indians, demonstrating that even when the relations between the two peoples were strained, personal relationship could be on good footing.

Daniel first hunted with carved pointed sticks with which he killed small animals like rabbits, possums and squirrels. He did not kill just for the sport of it but always dressed and cooked the meat for his family. He cleaned the hides and sold or traded them. Hunting and trapping became his livelihood, and the need to do this always drove him farther from civilization to find more animals. Buckskin quickly became the favorite clothing of hunters because it kept them warm and was very durable. So many hunters traded buckskins that the word "buck" came to be used for the Spanish dollar, the price of one hide. Dollars are still often referred to as "bucks" for this reason.

Daniel would later recall he was almost thirteen when he got his first rifle, no doubt made and given to him by his dad. Squire had developed gunsmith skills that he also passed on to his sons. Legend is that Daniel referred to his rifle by the name "Ticklicker," supposedly because he could shoot a tick off an animal without hurting the host. He competed in sharpshooter contests and won frequently. His new weapon allowed him to hunt turkeys in an area he referred to as the Flying Hills because of the abundance of the birds there to be hunted. Having only hunted animals on the ground before, it is easy to imagine how excited he was to now be able to shoot into the sky at birds as well. This literally opened up a whole new range of animals for Daniel to hunt.

A TV program in the 1960s introduced Daniel Boone to a new generation of kids. Fess Parker, who played the lead role, always wore a coonskin cap, and the lyrics to the theme song stated that Boone was a "big man" and "as tall as a mountain." Hollywood's version of history left a visual image that had little bearing to the real man who was remembered as being of average height. The only real likeness of Daniel came late in his life in

1820, when he finally sat still long enough to have his portrait painted by Chester Harding, who, appropriately enough, had to hunt Boone down to paint him. Even in the wrinkled face of an elderly man, his adventurous spirit is still obvious in his eyes.

Daniel could not focus on hunting alone for long as a young man. In the summer of 1755, when Daniel was almost twenty-one years old, the French and Indian War was raging in the American colonies. One might mistakenly think the name indicates the French were fighting against the Indians, but just the opposite was true. The French troops were fighting alongside the Indians against the English colonists, who were claiming more and more of their hunting and trapping lands for settlement. Wars in history were usually given names from the perspective of the opposing side, such as the English calling this conflict by the names of the enemies, the French and the Indians. This conflict was part of a larger one between the English and the French in Europe that was called the Seven Years' War. It became the colonists' fight once the French and the Indians took advantage of the opportunity to claim territory here.

Daniel Boone jumped into this conflict when he joined up with Major Edward Dobbs's state militia and served as a wagoner (someone who supplied the troops with transportation by wagons, as the name implies) and sometimes blacksmith with the troops led by British General Edward Braddock as they attacked Fort Duquesne near present-day Pittsburgh. It did not go well for Braddock in the battle, and he later died of wounds he suffered when the regular British soldiers fled from the more ambushing style of the Indians and lost the battle. British military were trained to fight in the Continental style, where they lined up shoulder to shoulder, waited for the command "Ready, aim, fire" and then marched toward the enemy, who had most politely done the same on the other side of the battlefield. The Indians hid in the trees and shot at the troops while they were still marching toward the battleground.

While this old style of fighting that the British army still used then looks suicidal and ridiculous to moderns, it was based on old technology, where muskets had a short range and had to be reloaded after each shot, and lingering medieval rules of war. Everyone in Europe understood these codes, but no one had taught them to the Native Americans. The colonists learned the advantage of surprise attacks, which later became known as guerrilla warfare (from a Spanish term that means "little war" first used over thirty years later as the technique was employed by the Spanish troops against Napoleon).

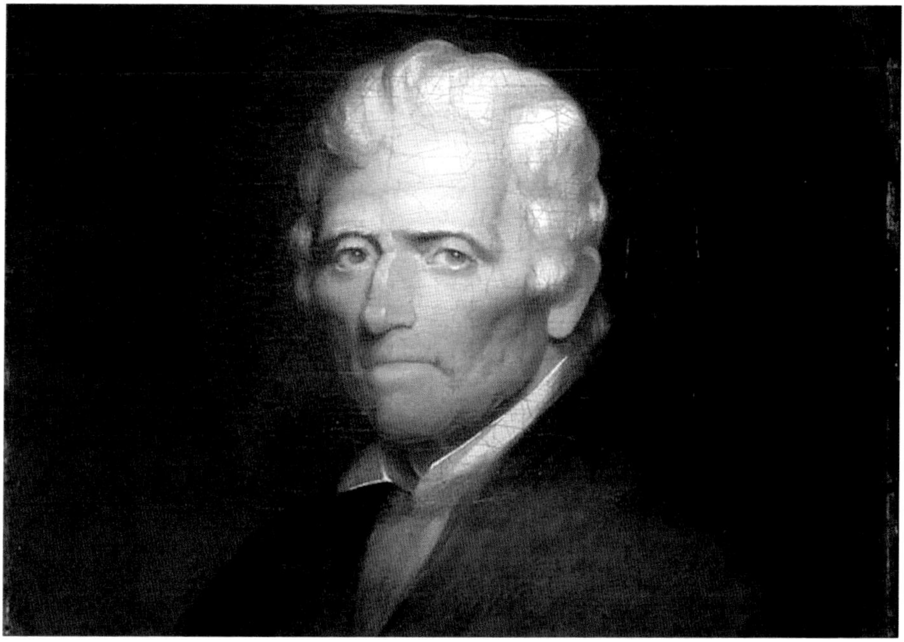

Chester Harding's 1820 portrait of Daniel Boone in the final year of his life. *Collection of the author.*

The smartest soldiers in the rear chose flight instead of fight when ambushed, and Daniel was one of them. He cut loose the horses in his charge and retreated with supplies so they could not be confiscated by the enemy. Often seen as an act of cowardice, a retreat such as Daniel's was a smart strategy when slaughter and scalping was all that lay ahead and the battle was already lost. The battle left a lasting impression on Daniel, as he returned to his homestead beside Bear Creek, relieved to be alive (and still in possession of his scalp) and to keep his favorite horses. It is possible he served as a ranger defending Fort Dobbs against Indian attacks, but mostly he defended his home. In his wartime involvement, he had gained a healthy respect for (and fear of) the Indians and a love of the mountains that he had traveled between North Carolina and western Pennsylvania.

General Braddock also had George Washington as his second lieutenant, and it is possible that Boone and Washington interacted in this campaign in their early twenties before either became famous. Washington survived two horses being shot from underneath him and his coat was grazed by four musket balls, but he was spared, as he later said, by "Providence."

More importantly to Daniel Boone's future life, he became friends with an Irish trader named John Findlay (sometimes spelled Findley or Finley), who told Boone of lands Findlay had explored on the other side of the mountains in a land called *kentak ee* (meaning land of meadows) by the Indians. The Irishman described fertile lands full of wildlife—all Boone needed to hear to be intrigued. Findlay even told the young man that he believed the area could be reached from North Carolina through a natural passageway in the mountains in the valley where the Cumberland River ran. Boone returned to the beautiful rolling hills of home, having learned a lot but also with an insatiable curiosity about what lay beyond those hills. He was convinced he no longer wanted to be a soldier, but now he was a wiser hunter and a more knowledgeable explorer.

Daniel did not have to hunt far to find his wife, a neighbor named Rebecca Bryan, the granddaughter of that early settler Morgan Bryan. Boone first met Rebecca at his sister's wedding. There is no proof to the old legend that he almost shot her while hunting, but it is easy to imagine he might have frightened her with his unusual ways of wandering off with a gun. While there is no portrait of Rebecca, she was described as tall and dark-haired, and by all accounts she was every bit as brave and strong as Daniel yet more steady. She no doubt had the Scots-Irish face so common now to Appalachian women, one with strong features etched into fair skin and looking out through expressive eyes. The young man who did not like to stay in one place for long found a mate he wanted to stay with and who was up to the challenge he would give her in life.

The couple's wedding in 1756 was officiated by his father, Squire Boone, who was a justice of the peace. Daniel was twenty-two years old and Rebecca was seventeen when they married and moved into a cabin on the Bear Creek property. Later, Squire deeded that property to Daniel, and the young man attempted to make it home and farm it.

Almost immediately after being married, Daniel and Rebecca adopted two of his nephews, Jesse and Jonathan, the orphaned sons of his brother Israel. Life was fragile on the frontier, and Daniel's brother had fallen ill with a fever. In spite of being taken to be treated by a doctor in the nearby Moravian settlement of Bethabara, Israel Boone died of consumption only a few months after his wife's death. Daniel and Rebecca raised the two boys as their own. In addition, they would have ten children of their own, so Rebecca had many mouths to feed as Daniel went off to hunt meat for them. It is clear from these facts that Daniel Boone struggled with grief and loss as a young man as well as encountered happiness. It is easy to imagine him deep in thought as he sought solace in the quiet woods and deep ravines where no other humans were treading.

Far less is known about Rebecca Boone than her famous husband. There is indication that Rebecca did not know how to read or write, marking deeds with an "X" in place of a signature. No historical record is needed to know she worked hard when she shouldered the responsibility for a large family of many children and often did it alone when Daniel was off on a long hunt. Months and sometimes even years would pass before he returned, and in addition to the work of the average woman in colonial America who cooked from scratch, sewed and washed clothes by hand, gardened and tended to animals, she also had to hunt for their food when the other hunter in the family was gone. Undoubtedly, she spent many nights wondering if something had happened to him and she was a widow and just did not know it yet. She had to be a strong woman in many ways.

Daniel Boone became disillusioned with formal religion after his family's experience with the Quakers and never again attended a church regularly, although he maintained a habit of daily Bible reading. Revival meetings were sweeping the frontier during this time, as the First Great Awakening waned and the Second Great Awakening was beginning. Circuit-riding preachers

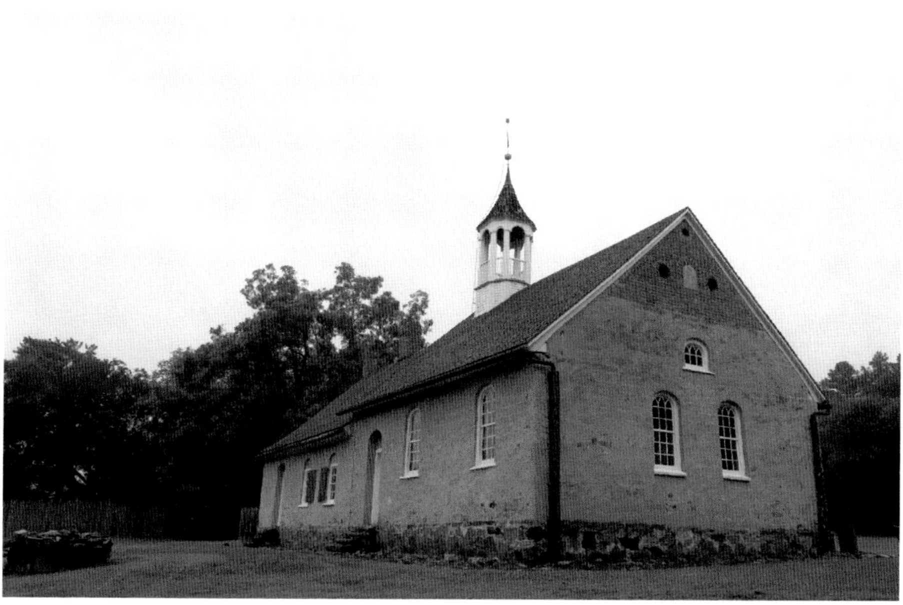

Bethabara, nearby Moravian settlement, where a doctor tended to Israel Boone at his death. *Collection of the author.*

like Francis Asbury were common, and many Baptist and Methodist churches began to spring up in small communities. Daniel attended these for communion and asked for his children to be baptized in several local Baptist churches. Faith permeated the colonial culture of the backwoods, with the sounds of fire and brimstone preaching and soft hymn humming accompanied by the strumming of stringed instruments. He could not have escaped this spiritual influence but did not commit to a congregation. His son Nathan would later tell his biographer Lyman Draper that his dad's "worship was in secret and he placed his hopes in the Savior." The last letter in Daniel's handwriting to his sister-in-law, who many believe had taught him to read years earlier, stated that "all the Relegan I have to love and fear God, believe in Jeses Christ, Dow all the good to my Nighbour and my Self that I Can, and Do as Little harm as I Can help, and Trust on gods marcy for the rest." Years later on his deathbed, his last words also expressed his confidence in the mercy of God.

His academic education was also sketchy, which accounts for his irregular spelling and lettering, but he was not illiterate and often was found reading literary classics by the light of campfire that further fired his sense of adventure. He was later sometimes the only literate person in gatherings on the frontier of Kentucky and was known for reading aloud to others at campfire gatherings. Campfires often served as a reading lamp. Fires were an essential part of life in colonial America on an everyday basis, obviously for heat and cooking but also as a source of light, whether in a fireplace on an early, still dark morning; on a tallow or beeswax candle; or from a campfire. Travelers would carry a tinder box with them containing a piece of steel specifically designed with a handle for starting a fire by means of flint and steel. Any sharp rock would be struck against the steel to create a spark that would set some kindling afire. Safety matches would not be commonly available for another century.

Books were a rare and valuable treasure in the eighteenth century. There were no public libraries, and bookstores were only in the largest eastern cities. Books had been printed on a printing press for three hundred years but were still printed on cloth rag paper (more like our paper money today) and bound with leather covers. They were hard to come by and costly to buy so were treated with respect and care. That was just the physical part. Inside the covers, they offered information (not as readily available as today with the Internet) and adventure as stories of other places and events inspired imagination. The most widely printed and owned book was, as it had been since the first printed Gutenberg copy, the Holy Bible.

In 1759, the Cherokee Wars threatened the safety of many settlers, and some chose to seek protection at Fort Dobbs in the neighboring county. The Boones actually retreated for several months to Virginia but returned to their North Carolina home as soon as thought to be safe. It is significant that the nature of Daniel Boone's relationship with the Indians was often friendly and peaceful but also marked by violent outbursts like this one.

Daniel tried his hand at farming and did various other jobs but loved none in comparison with hunting and trapping. However, it was tough making a living doing that alone. Daniel's name shows up often in court cases recorded in the county seat of Salisbury for debts he owed. He conducted a lot of business and answered several court summons in the county seat at the time. Only a few years later, a law clerk by the name of Andrew Jackson studied and practiced law in the same town of Salisbury before later becoming the war hero of the War of 1812 and then the first president of the United States from west of the Appalachian Mountains that Daniel was just beginning to explore.

Boone claimed increasing settlement forced him to travel farther afield toward the mountains to find the animals he needed to hunt to trade hides to

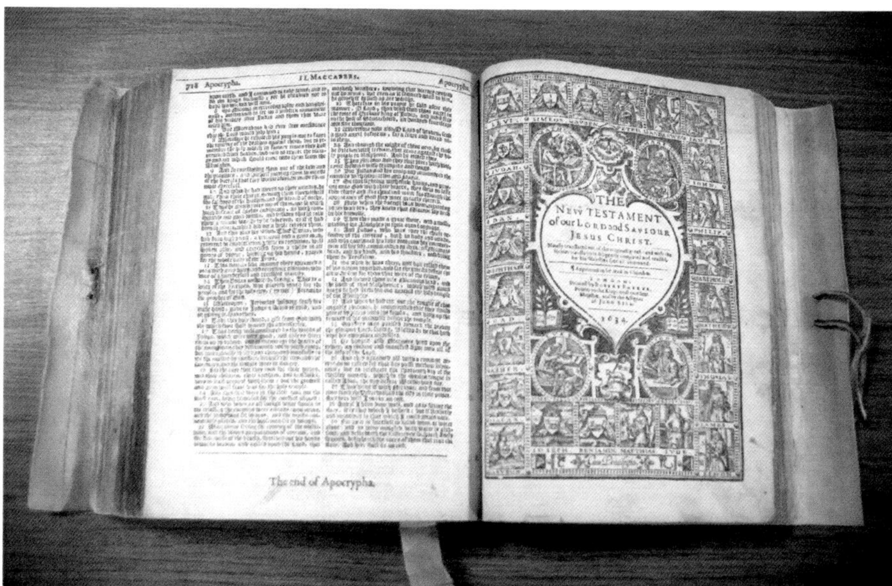


A seventeenth-century Bible similar to one Boone would have read. *Collection of Piedmont International University.*

pay off debts, but it was obvious he immensely enjoyed traipsing through the deserted woods alone. He could escape the growing population near his home and also his debts by hunting. The solution pleased him on both accounts. For all of his adult life, he moved on as soon as a place felt crowded. It would prove rare that he participated in the organization of a community into a town, and even his beloved Fort Boonesborough (first called Boone's Station and the first white settlement west of the mountains) later in Kentucky could only hold him for a few years. (Ironically, this community would later shrink away and is not an incorporated township even today. Boone would have been pleased.) He simply never liked to live where there were more people than animals and quickly moved farther into the wilderness, which on the gradually shrinking American frontier was almost always westward at that time.

Legend tells that sometime in 1760, he hunted for the first time on the other side of the mountains and left his mark in a tree near Gray, Tennessee. The inscription read:

*D.Boon*
*Cilled a Bar on tree*
*in the*
*year*
*1760*

The tree stood until a storm took it down in 1920, and the poor spelling and similarity to engraving on his father's tombstone indicated Daniel may have actually done it himself. However, thousands of markings similar to these have appeared on trees in the years since, some on trees too young to have been alive when Boone was, as copycats left their own marks. It seems impossible to prove which, if any, of these tree carvings are legitimate Daniel Boone relics.

Occasional hunting trips were not enough for the restless explorer. He quickly realized that the life of farming was not for him, so he sold the land by Bear Creek and moved on. Daniel Boone left Davie County (owing a few outstanding debts he continued to pay off over the years) and a large extended family in his thirties after spending his youth here. Those years were the most formative and important of his life. He had arrived as a teenager (although that is not a term they used then), learned the life skills necessary to support himself, found his wife and started a family of his own. It had been a safe place from which he launched his

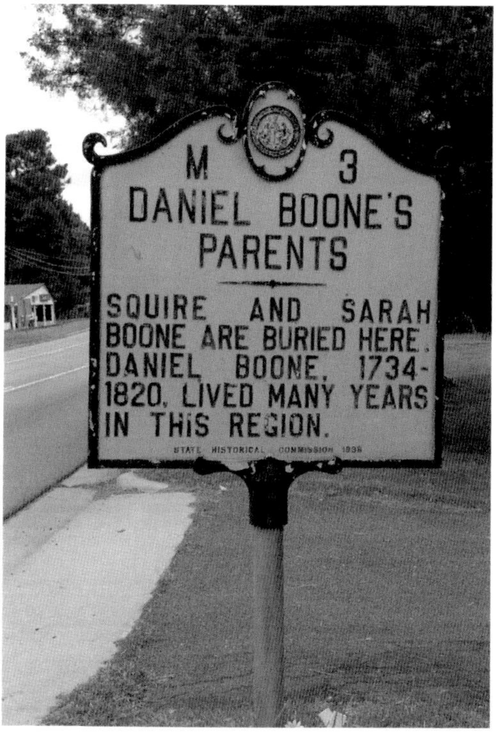


Historical marker on U.S. Highway 601 at Joppa Cemetery. *Collection of the author.*

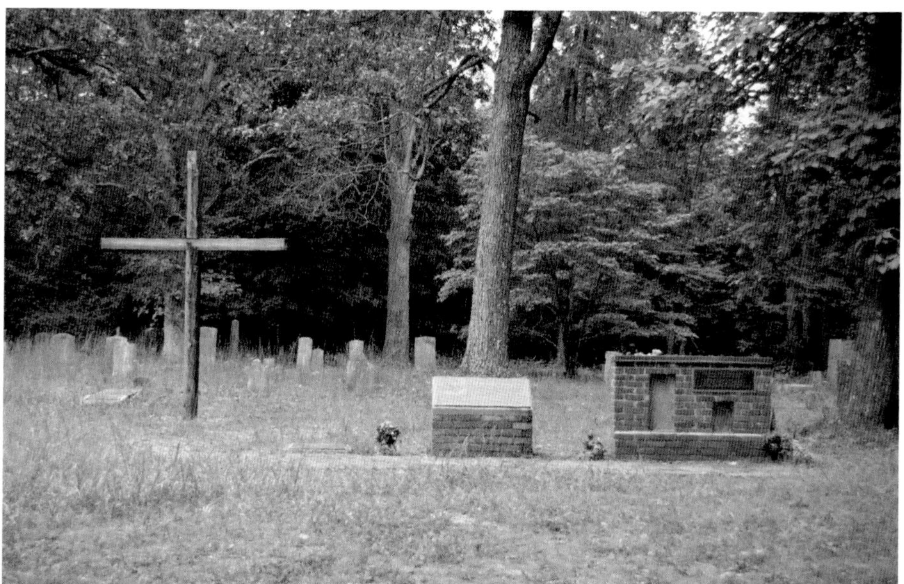

Oldest portion of Joppa Cemetery with the Boone family graves. *Collection of the author.*

hunting trips, part work and part exploration. It was, however, inevitable he would move on.

Daniel explored Florida with one of his brothers (and even bought a piece of land in the panhandle), but his ever-resilient wife refused to go there. Rebecca did not think the swamps of Florida a suitable place to raise a family, and Daniel must have listened to her. Apparently, she would not go with him and he would not go without her. Although Boone's legend is that of being a loner, it is noteworthy that he never left his family to escape them, as indicated often by his own words.

On the second day of 1765, Daniel's father, Squire Boone, died and was buried in Burying Ground Ridge, now called Joppa Cemetery, on the outskirts of Mocksville (then still referred to as Mocks Old Field) and just down the road or perhaps (some local historians believe) even on some of Squire's own property. Daniel's parents' graves are clearly marked there today by stones reported to have come from the Bear Creek farm. Squire's tombstone, probably the oldest in the county, bears the inscription that many believe, due to handwriting and poor spelling comparisons, Daniel carved himself:

> *Squire Boone*
> *Departed*
> *this life in*
> *they* [sic] *sixty*
> *ninth year*
> *of his age in*
> *they* [sic] *year*
> *of our Lord*
> *1765 Gene*
> *ary tha 2* [assumed to be a crude spelling of January the 2nd].

Sometime during 1766, Daniel moved his family up the Yadkin River about sixty-five miles to the Brushy Mountains for the winter. They would move several more times in North Carolina while Daniel made hunting trips farther and farther into the mountains to the west. Perhaps because he was gone for two years on the final such hunt, Rebecca and the children relocated with him to Kentucky.

Daniel often camped in the western mountains of North Carolina near the Watauga community, a group of Scots-Irish rebels who had fled the eastern part of the colony after the Battle of Alamance to avoid being

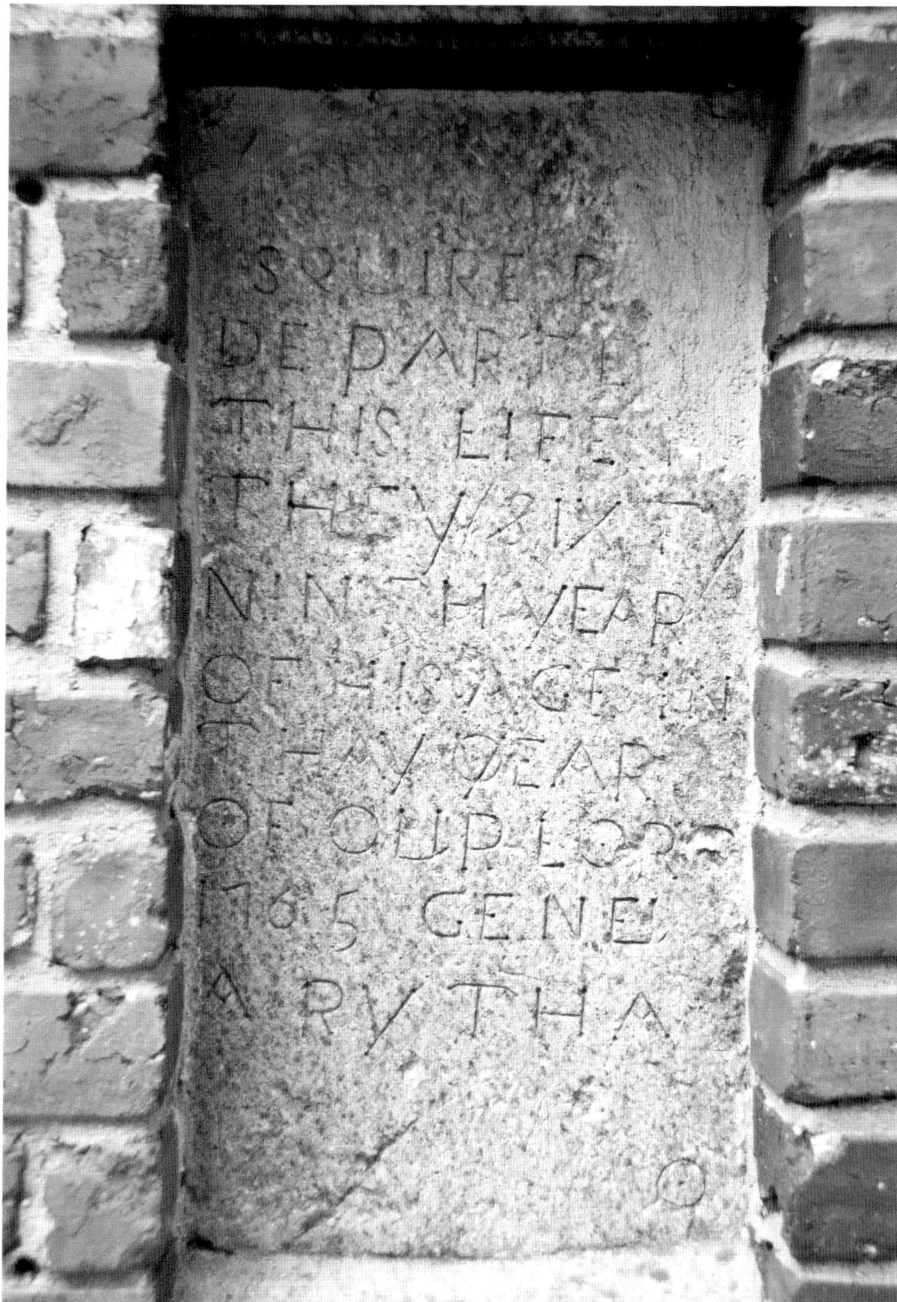


Squire Boone's tombstone, believed to be carved by his son Daniel. *Collection of the author.*

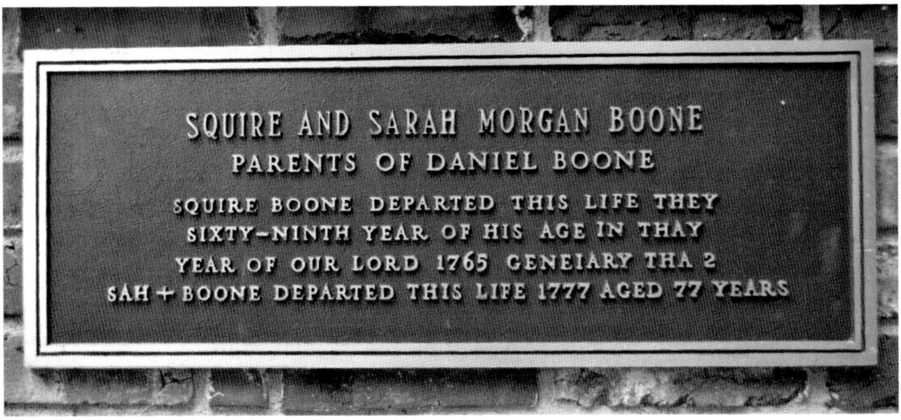


Marker with transcription of words on Squire Boone tombstone. *Collection of the author.*

controlled by the colonial government. They had fought the establishment, the British government, over taxes in the War of the Regulation that many historians consider to be the harbinger of the American Revolutionary War. Having been defeated in that conflict, they were often referred to as the Lost Province, as they hid out in a valley between the hills as the struggles escalated for land between the whites and the Indians and for power between the English and the colonists. Being Irish, they did not care who was in control in the governing bodies in the east, as long as they were left alone by them. This was the origins of the North Carolina town of Boone, named in honor of its frequent visitor and kindred spirit in their search for isolation. Daniel's two nephews, Jesse and Jonathan Boone, whom he had raised after their father Israel's death, lived there and were among the early members of one of the first churches in the area, Three Forks Baptist Church, still functioning today as a congregation. An outdoor drama, *Horn in the West*, has for sixty-six years depicted the conflict and community that forged the town of Boone, which today is home to Appalachian State University and hosts several monuments to Daniel Boone. The town of Boone famously claims that "the spirit of Daniel Boone still walks these mountains."

While serving in the French and Indian War, Daniel had heard of a place called the Cumberland Gap and the land of Kentucky, so instead of going south, he took his family north and west after expressing his determination to find a place of paradise for his family. Finding paradise was not easy, but he was not alone in his desire for it. A chance meeting with his old friend John Findlay, who knew the location of the gap in the mountains, motivated him to hunt a place instead of animals. He eventually led many others through the Cumberland Gap, including future president Abraham Lincoln's grandfather, after whom the more famous one would be named, and a cousin by marriage to Daniel. President Abraham Lincoln was shaped by his upbringing in the Midwest because Daniel Boone led his family there to a new way of life. Thousands of family stories took a turn west following Boone's leadership, and the Midwest went from wild, uncharted, fertile land to settled farmland much like the Carolinas. Boone, more than anyone, pointed the way to the promised land west of the mountains. His skills opened up clearings for homes and his courage inspired the next mass migration into the ever-shrinking frontier. He may not have been a founding father, but to colonial Americans, he was the dad who planned the road trip and then answered the question "Are we there yet?"

The Cumberland Gap is a natural pass through the Appalachian Mountain Range. The view from the Cumberland Gap National Historical Park in Middlesboro, Kentucky, makes it plain to see how it stretches out like a highway and beautiful alternative to crossing the mountains the hard way. Boone did not discover it, however, as is often the perception. It was first noted in public by a Virginia physician, Dr. Thomas Walker, in 1750, when Daniel Boone was only sixteen and not yet living in North Carolina.

The push of more settlers crowding in and the pull of a trip through the Cumberland Gap with his old friend Findlay drew Daniel to new unsettled lands. It is believed he said a tearful goodbye to his beloved mother and his siblings and headed west. The family migration was gradual and the dates of various stops along the way are not clearly recorded, but the birth of Daniel and Rebecca's youngest child, Nathan, in 1781 confirmed they had made it to Kentucky by then. Nathan Boone was the first white child known to be born in the new territory.

The Daughters of the American Revolution a century ago traced the path of Daniel Boone and erected numerous monuments on what is still referred to as Daniel Boone Heritage Trail. It links Virginia, North Carolina, Tennessee and Kentucky and marks the physical locations where Boone passed and left his mark. There is also a Daniel Boone Heritage Canoe Trail that begins near Boone's Cave. One can now follow Boone by land or by water.

Many trials (including the violent deaths of his brother-in-law and two sons and the kidnapping of his daughter at the hands of the Indians, as

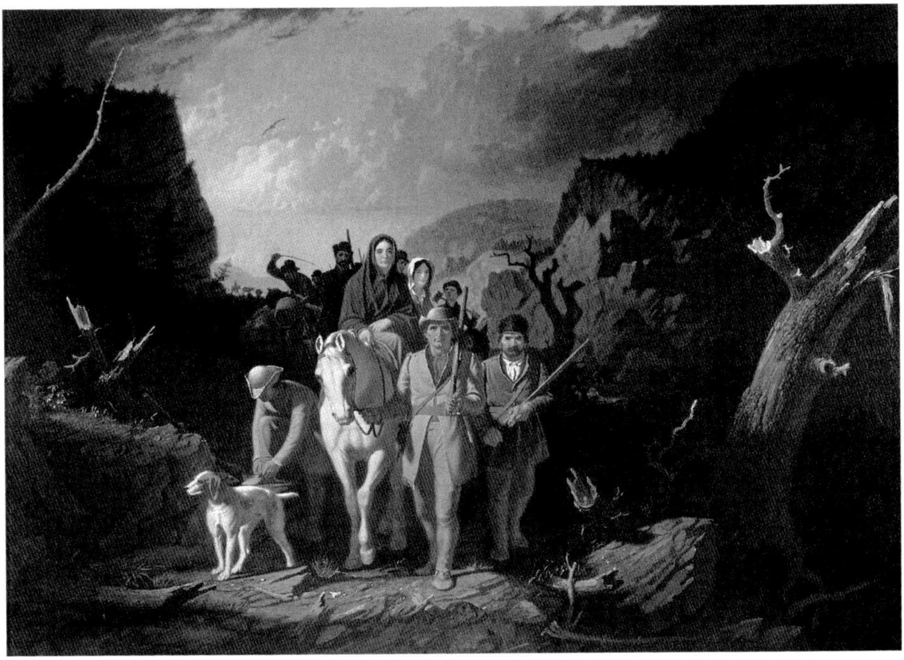

George Caleb Bingham's painting of Daniel Boone leading settlers through the Cumberland Gap. *Collection of the author.*

well as his own kidnapping and later a court-martial) and repeated moves lay ahead of Daniel Boone, but behind him was the countryside of his youth. He left British colonies and explored unsettled territories while the American Revolutionary War was taking place in the East. He became a citizen of the new nation even as he seemed to chase the setting sun on the western horizon.

Daniel's trail took him ultimately to Missouri, where he died in 1820, remarkably of old age (eighty-five) given his dangerous life (by which time he was such a living legend that he said he had read of his own death three times), having not only found the path to the West but led the way across it for many. He said of himself, "I am no Statesman. I am a Woodsman and think My Self...Capable of Making and Cutting that Rode." That road began along Bear Creek for the Great Pathfinder.

Daniel Boone left his footprints and name across the countryside he traveled. From the town of Boone in North Carolina (which has the distinction of being the highest elevation of any town of ten-thousand-plus population east of the Mississippi River, showing how ruggedly high the mountains were that faced him) to the Boone Falls in Tennessee, where legend says he hid behind the waterfall to escape Indians, every place seems to want to claim him. But none can claim him more than Davie County, North Carolina, where he learned his woodsman skills, left many relatives and struck out on his exploration of the American frontier that lay to the west. When he truly left home for his life's work, that home was here.

While the thirteen colonies focused on winning independence from England and then forming a new republic as a nation, Boone gave leadership to a great surge of migration across the mountains into the western frontier lands. The newly formed United States of America only numbered thirteen states in 1776 but by the beginning of the 1800s had added the western states of Kentucky, Tennessee and Ohio. Daniel Boone played a critical role in their settlement.

To a large degree, winning the American Revolutionary War had been possible because the thirteen colonies were contained by the mountains along the Eastern Seaboard, close enough to one another to work together and withstand the British army. The Patriots had won the war and the support of the backcountry North Carolinians, who named a nearby town Lexington in honor of the place where the war began in Lexington, Massachusetts. By the time the war was won, Boone had led countless settlers through the mountains and walked in the lead into the next chapter of American history, that of westward expansion.

Interestingly, Boone's body continued to travel after his death in 1820 in Missouri at his son Nathan's home. Kentucky very much wanted him to be buried on its soil and later moved what it believed were his and Rebecca's bones to a grave in that state. Both states still claim to have his grave site, so even today there is a bit of mystery surrounding the man who never stayed in any place for long and owned no land in his own name when he died. There is no reason to believe he ever returned to North Carolina after 1779 and the place that fostered his sense of adventure and taught him the survival skills he used the remainder of his life, but he clearly took with him what he had learned here.

Boone's legendary fame was not limited to Americans. He inspired British poet Lord Byron (himself rushing into the Greek War of Independence in search of his own heroic legend and ultimately meeting a premature death), who devoted seven stanzas in his 1823 epic piece of writing *Don Juan* to praising Daniel Boone in lines like the following:

*'T is true he shrank from men even of his nation,—*
*When they build up unto his darling trees,*
*He moved some hundred miles off, for a station*
*Where there were fewer houses and more ease;*
*The inconvenience of civilisation*
*Is, that you neither can be pleased nor please;*
*But where he met the individual man,*
*He showed himself as kind as mortal can.*

Daniel Boone's contribution to American history is well known. He did not discover the Cumberland Gap, but he led the charge through it that opened up the territory west of the Appalachian Mountains to settlement by Americans. The new nation looking for new space found its leader in a fearless explorer. He was a loner who was followed by thousands. He was a private man who became a legend during his lifetime in an era without modern media to create a celebrity. He was a hunter and trapper who personified the American rugged individualist who became identified with the West. He was a pioneer and adventurer who physically led the way west and became the role model of how to conquer a national wilderness. He was the ultimate maverick.

*Chapter 4*

# HINTON HELPER

Nine years after Daniel Boone died in distant Missouri, a baby named Hinton Rowan Helper was born to Daniel and Sarah Helper on December 27, 1829, on the former Boone farm beside Bear Creek, where the original Boone family log cabin was still standing. Oddly, the baby was given the middle name of the county at the time he was born, Rowan, but during his childhood, the area became the newly created Davie County. This was symbolic of his life, born into one era and living into another.

Incidentally, Daniel Boone did not have a middle name, but Helper was born during the era when giving middle names at birth was becoming more common. (Hinton's brother Hanson, who later ran the Helper Hotel in Davidson, was given the middle name of Pinckney and lived life with the nickname "Pink" or "Pink Helper" and even "Mr. Pink.") The term "middle name" first appeared in print in the 1830s in a Harvard University publication. Prior to that, only the elite or royalty (who still take it to the extreme, causing Princess Diana's famous stumble during her wedding vows) inserted additional names to prove lineage. So for years middle names came from family links or place of origin, like Helper's did. Others were given the name of a person of honor, hence why so many men born in the United States in the 1800s were named George Washington before the surname, including George Washington Carver and the author's great-grandfather George Washington McClamrock. World War I enlistment forms were the first official documents to require a middle name, so many entering military service in the twentieth century had to choose their own middle name on the spot, as did the author's stepdad and uncle Tag Bowers, the latter of whom wrote "None" on the blank provided for middle name and "N" became his legal middle initial. Most United States presidents prior to the twentieth century did not have middle names, including George Washington and Abraham Lincoln, and the last president not to have a middle name was the first of the twentieth century, Theodore Roosevelt, although Harry S Truman did have just a middle initial. In the twentieth century, it became fashionable for presidents to often be referred to by their three initials, such as FDR and JFK, something that would not have been possible before.

The old Boone cabin that the Daniel Helper family first used stood on that spot until the 1920s. It continued to be used as an outdoor kitchen for many years. Outdoor kitchens were quite common in the South before air conditioning. If the open fire they cooked over spread, only the kitchen was lost and not the entire home. After all, there was no fire department down the road like there is now. The cabin Daniel Helper built for his family is still standing there, now encased in modern siding but with some of the original

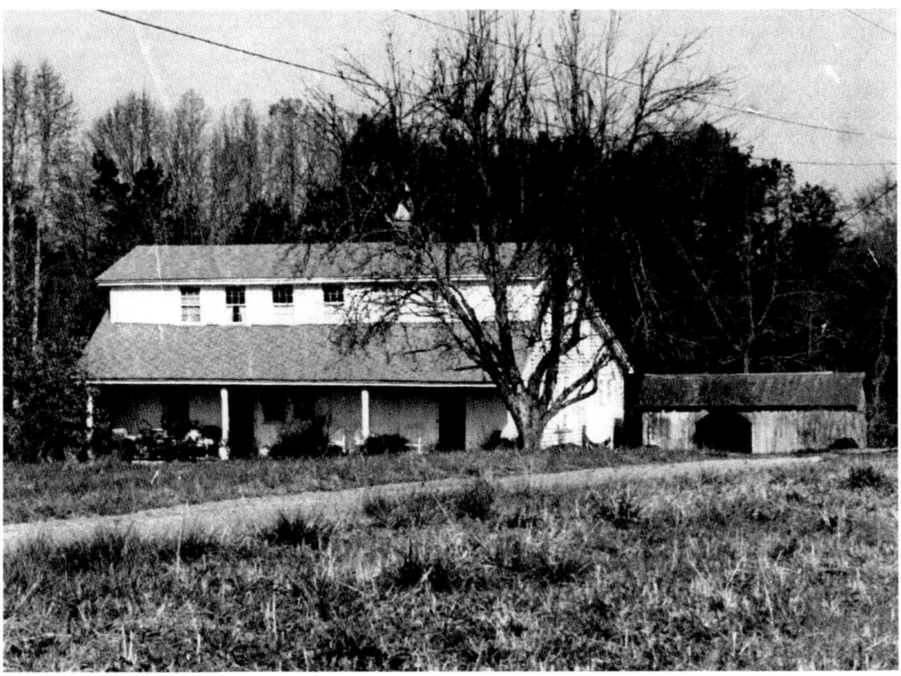

A twentieth-century photograph of the house in which Hinton Helper was born. *Collection of the Davie County Public Library.*

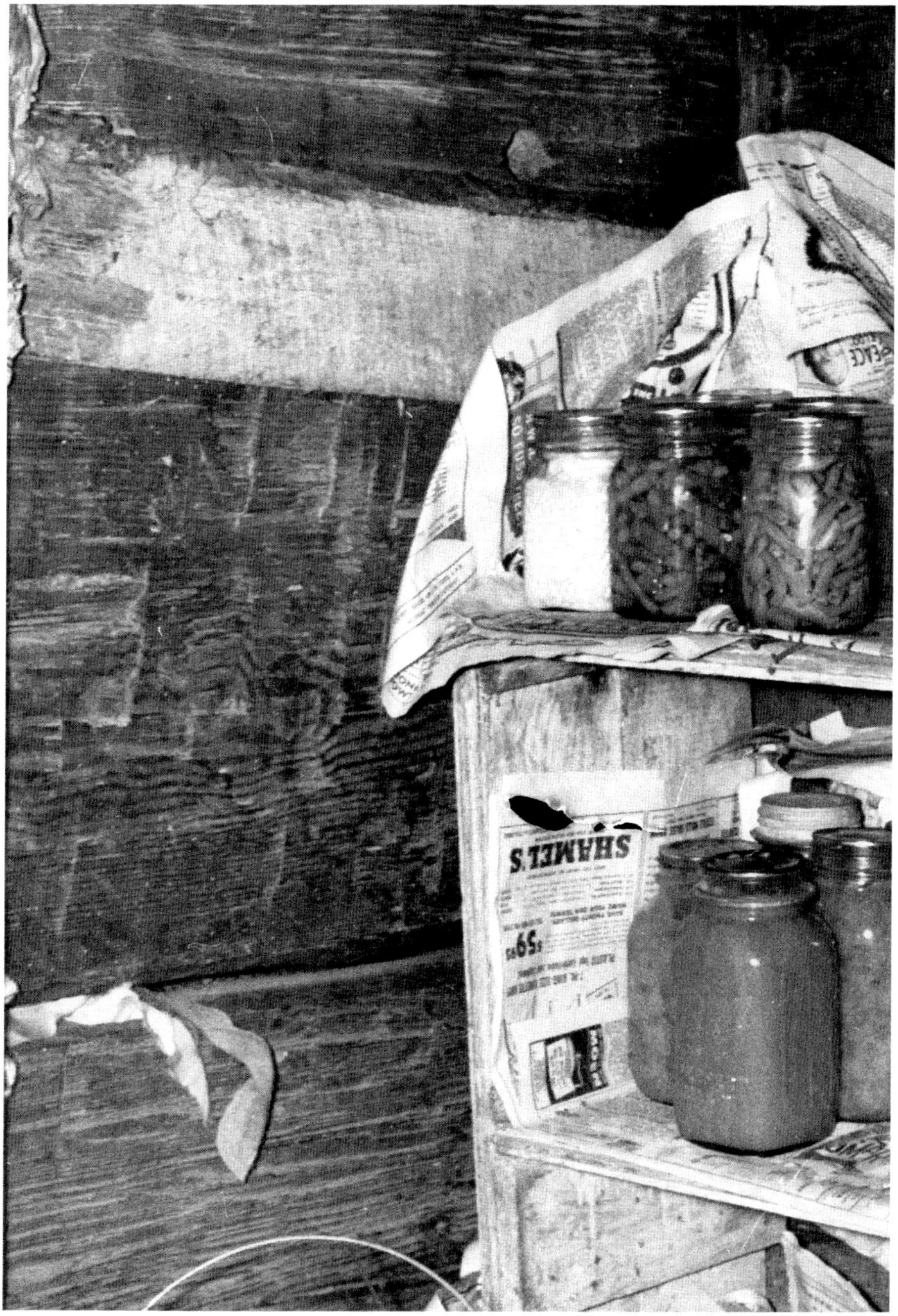

A twentieth-century photograph of original cabin logs within the Helper House. *Collection of the Davie County Public Library.*

logs visible. Some of the logs may have been reused from an original Boone structure, as there had been two such cabins when they lived there. This is not unusual; many small homes in Davie County are actually original log cabins still intact but hidden behind modern siding. That can often be visually detected by the small size and unusual placement of the windows.

The land itself had changed little during those years since Daniel Boone had left. The county name had been changed to Davie, but that was an administrative decision made far away. The new county seat and town of Mocksville (originally Mock's Old Field, but Mr. Mock did not leave a lot of information about himself to history) would be incorporated in 1839, a decade after Hinton's birth. Many more settlers had arrived, however, and Daniel Boone's instincts that the land was filling up were being proven right.

Hinton Helper's father was a slave owner who farmed two hundred acres, but he did not leave much of an impression on the boy, as his father died when Hinton was less than one year old. Hinton could not remember his father but recalled well by name the four slaves his father had owned: Judy, Joe, Jinsy and Jack. It is highly likely the absence of his father but the presence of his slaves shaped Hinton's upbringing and thinking.

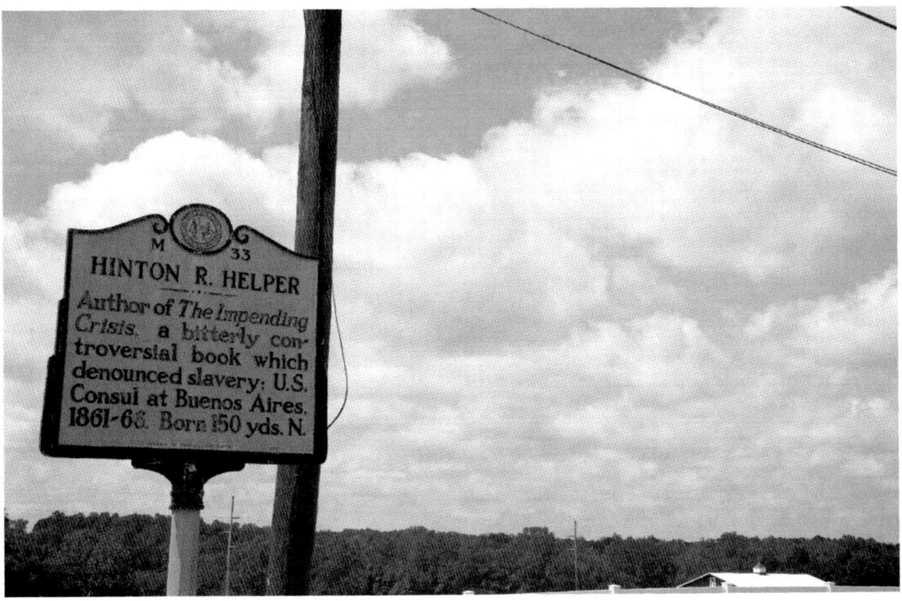


Hinton Helper historic marker on U.S. Highway 64. *Collection of the author.*

Not a lot is known about the childhood of the only one of these boys to spend his entire boyhood on the land beside Bear Creek. (The autobiographical references in his own later writings are questionable as to whether they are reliable, as much of his writing was proven to not be.) He often recalled plowing fields, so apparently he worked on the family farm while growing up. It is hard to imagine he did not play on the creek bank and run the fields beside it in any free time, as all boys would. There is record he had three older siblings die while he was a young boy, so his childhood was also marked by death and sadness. Death at a young age was far more common then and for most of history than it is today. Just wander through any old cemetery for proof. The life expectancy in 1830 in America was around age forty. Many lived much longer (as had Boone decades before), but the number was lowered by the high death rate of infants and small children as disease and lack of modern medicine such as vaccines took their toll on the weakest.

In the absence of his father, Hinton was raised and encouraged by a large extended family in the area. His grandfather Jacob Helfer (whose last name was later changed in spelling to Hinton's surname of Helper and also to Hepler, which many local residents still go by) was Germanic and a man of means. He also was reportedly a Hessian soldier with Cornwallis's troops in the American Revolutionary War. Rowan County records show that he purchased a large portion of Squire Boone's former landholdings in 1795 and settled in to stay. Baptism records show the family members were associated with the Heidelberg Lutheran Church, not surprisingly, since the area was increasingly becoming a gathering of German immigrants. Helper's mother, Sarah Brown, came from an even more affluent neighboring family that referred to their dwelling as a mansion, and the family land was described as a plantation in her father's will in 1831, but that date means Hinton was also too young to know that grandfather.

Plantations and slave owners were not common in this area of Western North Carolina, so the family was clearly upper class when compared to their neighbors. Even so, years later Hinton would refer to his family as "poor white." Strong Quaker (like the Boones) and Moravian backgrounds among many of the other neighboring settlers caused the community to mostly reject slavery on a religious basis. Many more simply could not afford slaves. In the 1860 census, about one in five families owned slaves, but most only owned one and only a rare few owned many. The fact that Hinton Helper's family owned four slaves made them unusual in the area.

Not much is known about his father, but Hinton later wrote that he did not believe his dad had ever traveled more than twenty miles from his home in Davie County, very possibly true given his short life that ended at age thirty-five. His only known travel was to the town of Salisbury, twenty miles away. Hinton also noted that the methodical course of his father's mind determined that he and five of his siblings were given names that were alliterative, beginning with the letter "H," and only his sister Amanda's name was picked by his mother. Choices for first names at this time in history tended to reflect biblical names, often-repeated family names and very imaginative names like Hinton and his brothers Horace, Hardy, Hanson and Hampton and his sister Henney.

Hinton was greatly influenced by his uncle on his mother's side, Thomas Brown. He even became a Presbyterian like him. This uncle made sure he received a good education, beginning at the Mocksville Academy, a private school that catered to the wealthier families in the community. It was in this well-regarded school that Hinton was taught by a very unusual teacher named Peter Ney. Ney was known for his great knowledge of French history, fluency in many languages, equestrian skills, poetry writing and painting. One of the most unusual skills he demonstrated for his students was fencing, remarkable in the gun and knife culture of pre–Civil War Western North Carolina. Ney was a mysterious figure (discussed in the next chapter), but clearly his European style and perspective impacted a whole generation of impressionable boys (who undoubtedly knew no one else who wielded a sword and a flute equally well) in the classroom at Mocksville Academy. Hinton Helper was one of those boys, and no doubt his perspective on the world was widened by this unique individual in the otherwise small world of Davie County. Daniel Boone's curiosity always focused on the West and Tom Ferebee's focus would be on the sky, but Hinton's was turned toward the Old World in the eastern horizon by a very influential teacher.

After Hinton graduated from school in 1848, he began work as an apprentice to Michael Brown (not believed to be a relative), a bookshop owner in Salisbury and also a slave owner. This helped steer Hinton toward a life in books, not farming. He resembled his predecessor on the farm Daniel Boone in this respect of rejecting farming. Ironically, none of the three boys written about in this book took farming as his livelihood.

Apprenticeship was the normal route to learn a trade in the 1800s, as it had been for centuries since the Middle Ages in Europe. Without trade schools and community colleges like today, a young man between the ages of fourteen and twenty would contract to learn a skilled trade from a master

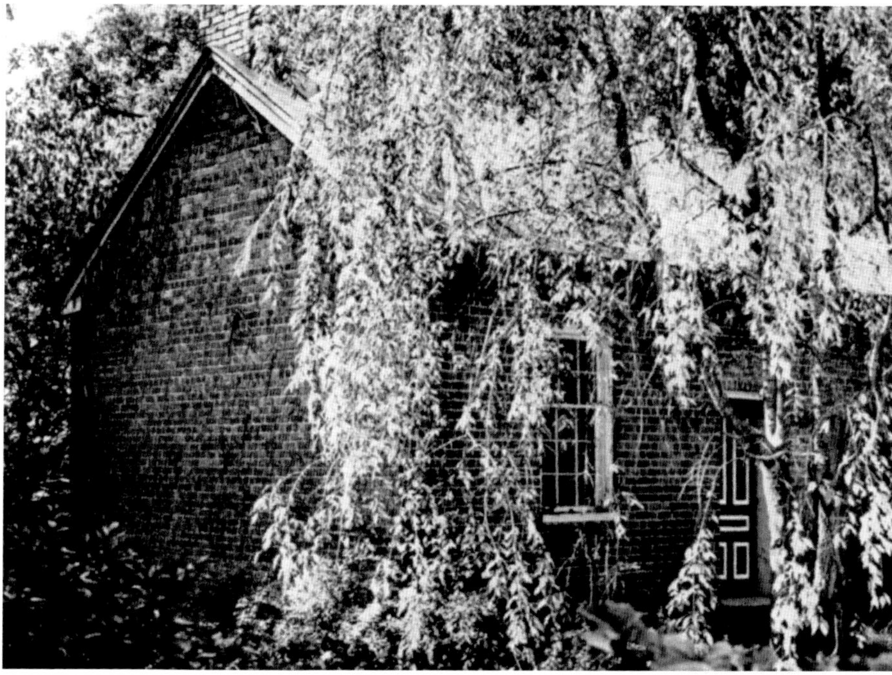

An old photograph of Mocksville Academy. *Collection of the Davie County Public Library.*

craftsman. He would agree in this written and signed contract to work for the master, and the master would agree to train him, normally for seven years. These contracts often included particular clauses, such as agreement not to divulge some of the master's secrets, such as where to find the best clay for pottery. These are still referred to today as "trade secrets," and business ethics dictate protecting them. At the end of the apprenticeship, the master would declare him a worthy tradesman, often giving him a new suit of clothing and then sending him on his way to be a journeyman who, as the term implied, traveled around offering his new services. The goal was to become capable enough to establish one's own shop as a master craftsman and train other apprentices.

After only a year as an apprentice, however, Hinton left Salisbury under a cloud of disgrace, having stolen $300 (an even larger sum in that day's economy) from the bookshop of his employer. Though he confessed and repaid it later, he never escaped the local label of being a thief. He might have become a bookshop owner in the booming town of Salisbury, but this turn of events took him elsewhere. Timing in history accounts for much. The lure of money drew him to his next adventure as word of the 1849 California gold rush took him west to the gold mines, along with many other young men seeking their fortune. The rush began when James Marshall discovered gold at Sutter's Mill in 1848, and as word reached the East Coast, over 300,000 men traveled west to the gold fields in the next few years. Hinton Helper was one of them, as he sailed on a clipper ship named the *Stag Hound* to the port of San Francisco. The chance to find gold and personal riches was one powerful motive for human migration. Thus, within a lifetime of when Daniel Boone had first led settlers through the Cumberland Gap to the western side of the Appalachian Mountains, men were traveling all the way to the West Coast of the continent. California became a state in 1850 due to this influx of population. Many such men, called Forty-Niners, like Helper, returned home disappointed, and few found gold. Others stayed and found their wealth in other ways, like James Folger, who sold ground coffee to the miners and whose name still is found on Folgers Coffee, and Levi Strauss, who made pants of a tough cloth for the miners called denim, the first use of the material of blue jeans.

Hinton worked the gold fields for several years but later claimed that he had made only ninety-three and three-quarters cents after working one mine for three months. He left no richer except for the experience of a chaotic life much different from his country one. He had left North Carolina for California as a young man just twenty-one years old and returned a man much more knowledgeable about the ways of the Wild West. He was also much disillusioned. He felt so strongly about what he had discovered instead of gold that upon returning to Salisbury, he wrote a book, *The Land of Gold: Reality Versus Fiction*, which criticized California for everything from its seedy lifestyle to the weather. Helper adopted an air of superiority in his written criticism of culture that became a reoccurring theme in his writing. He also used statistics as a purveyor of economic facts to make his case, and this also was a tool he would use again. Notable is the fact that in this book he praised the institution of slavery and believed it would be a good idea and profitable in new territory. It is likely, although not clearly stated by him, that his experience in a bookstore (he renewed his friendship with Michael Brown upon returning and paying off his debt) and his exposure to literature and life's disappointment at the hands of his teacher Peter Ney manifested itself in picking up a pen and writing. It was the first of many books he would author, almost all of which carry the same strongly negative emphasis. Again, timing was everything, as the East was hungry for information about the West. Helper's book about California was not a bestseller but sold enough to encourage him to become an author and cultural critic.

Timing was perfect for becoming an author. In the 1840s, there was a revolution in the technology of book publishing that made books far more common and affordable for mass distribution. It was the perfect storm of demand and supply. Once again, the Bible created the demand for mass printing as the revivals and the birth of organizations like the American Bible Society generated a widespread public desire for books. Supply was made possible by industry innovations that included steam as a source of power, mechanical typesetting, lithography and copyright laws. Free libraries opened everywhere, and instead of diminishing personal purchasing of books as feared, they proved to actually encourage it. This expanding book trade industry even radically changed the look and feel of a book, as the booming demand made leather harder to come by and books began to be covered by first cloth and then paper. Paper itself went from being made from cloth rags (similar to how our durable dollar bills are still made) to using wood pulp, as not enough cloth rags were available to meet the demand.

Hinton wrote a number of books, but the one written in the mid-1850s would become the most well known and controversial, as well as life changing for its author: *The Impending Crisis of the South.* Hinton Helper was about to face his own impending crisis.

*The Impending Crisis of the South: How to Meet It* was published in 1857, only four years before the Civil War began. Helper capitalized on timing yet again. He was still just in his twenties, but he sold his part of the family farm alongside Bear Creek to a brother and moved north to where the book publishing companies were located. As a farm boy from North Carolina, he had instant credibility to speak to the agricultural collapse of the South in the eyes of northerners. With an antislavery slant, he quickly became the darling of the abolitionists. As an educated man, he created multiple tables of statistics in his book to make the case that slavery would be the economic downfall of the South. In great detail, he compared things like population from the 1850 census and value per an acre of land in states in the North with states like North Carolina to prove economic decline during the seventy years prior to his time period. Even though the weight of his evidence was impressive, it was flawed in its accuracy, and therefore, the conclusions he drew from it were compromised. Davie County historian James Wall did a masterful job in his 1949 thesis of researching how Helper deliberately skewed the facts to prove his points. For example,

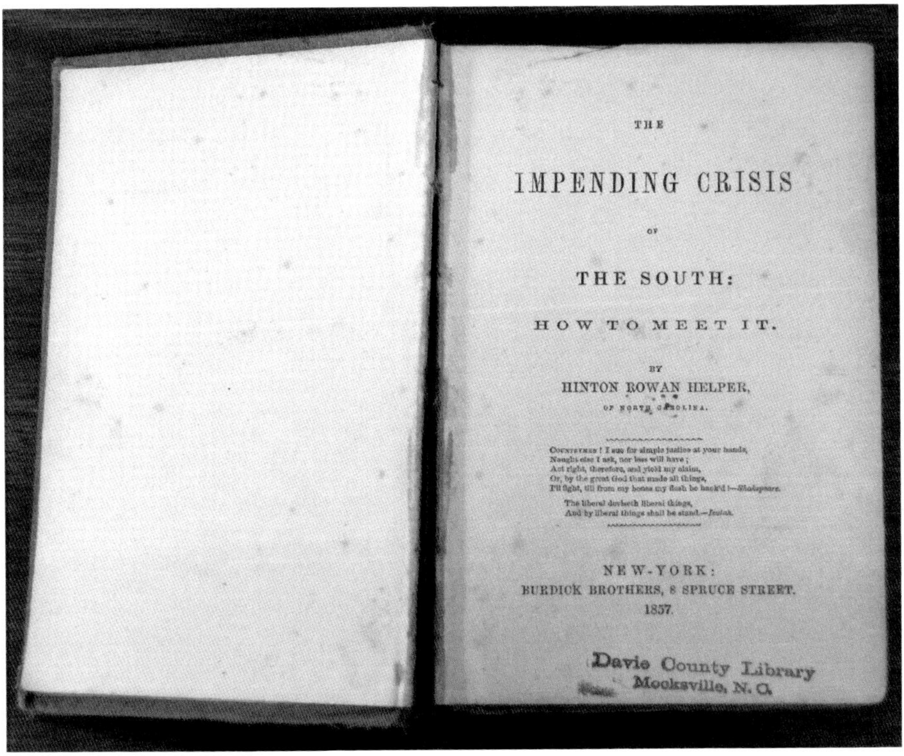


*The Impending Crisis* by Hinton Helper. *Collection of the author.*

Helper compared agricultural wealth between northern and southern states but did not include the four main cash crops of the South: cotton, tobacco, rice and sugar cane. The South had many more farms and was much richer in annual agricultural production than northern states, the opposite of his conclusions. A Davie County farm boy should have gotten that right. According to Wall, "He also used two different years in the same comparison in order to establish his 'proof'" and compared dissimilar states. Helper argued that the majority of farmers in the South were not slave owners and paid a huge price for the richest plantation owners, whom he called "lords of the lash," to succeed. He wrote in this book, "It is a fact well known to every intelligent Southerner that we are compelled to go to the North for almost every article of utility and adornment." The book so belabored statistics that it was a difficult read, and indeed, most people did not bother to read it, for a variety of reasons. But many did believe it was a truthful and accurate analysis; Helper had used facts to make a powerful case but mostly to his own advantage. The author's credibility might have been investigated and challenged had the nation not been swept up in its rush toward civil war.

Helper's book was dedicated to non-slaveholding whites. No doubt he believed he was being an advocate for his own people. He appealed to the poor in the South, but the timely publication of the book in New York (no one south of the Mason-Dixon line would dare print it) made it instead a tool of the abolitionists. Rare was the southerner who even saw the book before the Civil War broke out. One aged North Carolina Methodist minister named Daniel Worth of Guilford County was arrested and convicted of the crime of distributing the book as incendiary material, which was against the law in his home state. Hinton Helper had unknowingly cast his lot with the enemy and against his neighbors.

Helper's book sold well in the North, however, just prior to the 1860 election after it was mass produced in a condensed, more affordable form by the Republican Party and widely distributed as its primary campaign document. Some historians propose it might have been responsible for Abraham Lincoln's close election to the presidency, which changed American history significantly. It was second only to *Uncle Tom's Cabin* as literature that inflamed antislavery passion. Helper's work was nonfiction and cerebral, while the fictional *Uncle Tom's Cabin* was the bestselling novel in the United States in the 1800s. It remains a classic today as the tale of a runaway slave written by Harriet Beecher Stowe in 1852. A favorite among abolitionists, it humanized slavery in a very emotional way. Stowe, the daughter of well-known preacher Lyman Beecher and sister to Henry Ward Beecher, and a Massachusetts teacher who had never visited the South, based her novel on the life story of a runaway slave, Josiah Henson, who escaped to Dresden in Ontario, Canada, where a museum to him exists. The fictional account depicts the vicious master Simon Legree and the long-suffering slave Uncle Tom. In modern times, those names have come to represent racists and any African American who caters to whites, respectively. At the time just prior to the Civil War, her book moved many to sympathize with the slaves, and when President Abraham Lincoln later met Mrs. Stowe, he supposedly (although no documentation exists to support it) declared, "So this is the little woman who started the Great War." While Stowe's book stirred emotional response to the plight of the slaves, Helper's addressed the economic hazards of slavery to Southerners; his later racist writings revealed no sympathy to the enslaved. Stowe's book reached the heart while Helper's appealed to the mind (and the wallet).

Ironically, Hinton Helper left his native North Carolina for the Union and then North Carolina left the Union, joining the new nation of the Confederate States of America, even as Helper was heading for yet another country, Argentina. Confederates justified their separation from the United States on the basis of what the thirteen original colonies had done seventy-five years before in leaving their bond with England. A whole lot of leaving going on! Incidentally, the Civil War settled once and for all the question of whether the United States was a group of states with the power to join and leave the Union whenever they wished. This story is told in the use of one little verb. Prior to the Civil War, the name of the country was joined to a plural verb, as in "the United States are...," but since the Civil War, it is correct to state "the United States is..." with the single verb indicating one indivisible union.

Helper's incendiary book also sparked a heated debate on the floor of the United States Congress. John Sherman (brother of General William T. Sherman, who a few years later became famous for his March to the Sea and ultimately across North Carolina during the Civil War) was being considered as Speaker of the House, but his endorsement of *The Impending Crisis* incited members to come armed with weapons. Such free publicity for the book only helped its sales. Helper, however, told friends that he did not realize any profit from the sale of the book. The man who wrote a book about the bad business of slavery had apparently written a bad contract with his book agent. The furor over the book persisted into 1861, when a New York paper published broadsheets for distribution that blamed the bloodshed of the war on Helper. It seems he had enemies north and south of the Mason-Dixon line.

Unlike Boone, Hinton eagerly embraced getting an education and became a man of letters, a writer. Like Boone, he left the area as a young man to become a hero in another area, but unlike Boone, Hinton became hated in his home state. No towns in North Carolina are named Helper. During the Civil War, the state of North Carolina was divided in its loyalties to the Union and the Confederacy (one of Helper's brothers fought for the Union and a close childhood friend died as a Confederate soldier), and the state was filled with refugees fleeing to sympathetic areas, but nowhere in the state was there a place found for a man seen as a traitor to his home. Lack of loyalty was apparently the unforgivable sin.

Hinton Helper's lot in life and future career now lay with the Union. During the Lincoln administration, he was sent as a diplomat to Argentina (a job given as patronage but also to get him out of the national eye as the war began), where he met and married his wife, Maria Louisa Rodriguez. After

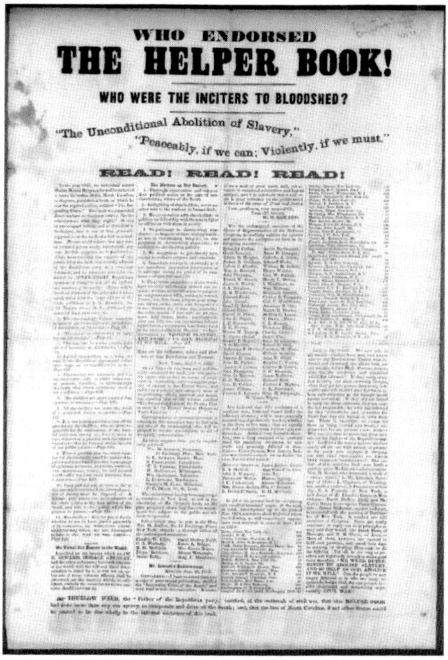

WHO ENDORSED

THE HELPER BOOK!

WHO WERE THE INCITERS TO BLOODSHED?

"The Unconditional Abolition of Slavery,"

"Peaceably, if we can; Violently, if we must."

READ! READ! READ!

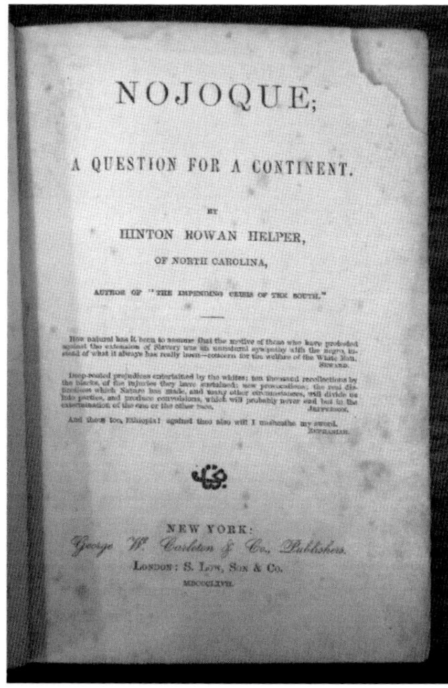

NOJOQUE;

A QUESTION FOR A CONTINENT.

BY

HINTON ROWAN HELPER,

OF NORTH CAROLINA,

AUTHOR OF "THE IMPENDING CRISIS OF THE SOUTH."

NEW YORK:

George W. Carleton & Co., Publishers.

LONDON: S. LOW, SON & CO.

MDCCCLXVII.

*Left*: An 1861 broadside condemning those who endorsed *The Impending Crisis. Collection of Museum of Early Southern Decorative Arts, Old Salem Museums and Gardens.*

*Right*: Cover page of Hinton Helper's book *Nojoque. Collection of the author.*

the war was over, he returned to briefly live in Asheville but found sentiment too strong against him in his own state to remain even in that remote mountain town, as it was then. He worked a number of different jobs and wrote more books, even three racist ones denouncing African Americans. His 1868 book *Negroes in Negroland* revealed he had very racist ideas about the former slaves. He was in no way a model abolitionist. The institution of slavery produced conflicted ideas among Southern whites in the mid-nineteenth century in America. Thomas Jefferson had said that dealing with slavery was like holding onto the ears of a wolf—a person cannot hang on but dare not let go. From the Civil War to the civil rights movement a century later and even still today, racial tension remains among Americans. In this regard, the past does not simply whisper to the present; it yells at it, and the present screams back.

In his 1867 book called *Nojoque, A Question for a Continent* (*Nojoque* is Portugese for "I do not care" but also implied another meaning with its pronunciation), he began with the following description of his origins alongside Bear Creek:

*What matters it that my father and mother, and brothers and sisters, and myself, were all born and reared in the good Old North State? What matters it that my father, who never saw, and scarcely ever heard of, a railroad, a steamer, or a telegraph, and who, without ever traveling more than twenty miles from home, owned land and slaves, and lived and died, on the eastern bank of Bear Creek, a small tributary of the South Yadkin, in the western part of North Carolina?*

His resolution to the race issue first appeared on the dedication page:

*That the most Enlightened and Progressive Portion of the People of the New World...Determine Irrevocably by their vote, in 1868–1872... that...no Slave nor Would-be Slave, No Negro nor Mulatto, No Chinaman nor unnative Indian, No Black nor Bi-colored Individual of Whatever Name or Nationality, shall ever again find Domicile anywhere Within the Boundaries of the United States of America.*

He proposed the following plan on page 15:

*By giving full and formal notice to the negroes—every one of them, including the mulattoes, the quadroons, the octoroons, and all the other non-whites, that, after the 4th of July, 1876, their presence would be no longer required nor tolerated north of the northern border of Mexico, and by assisting them to a limited extent, to get somewhere (it would matter very little where) south of that south-moving boundary.*

Helper was suggesting a removal of an entire race of people even after the Emancipation Proclamation had become law of the land and also by the date of the centennial celebration of the Declaration of Independence that declared all men were created equal.

He wrote in very disturbing wording the following: "We should so far yield to the evident designs and purposes of Providence, as to be both willing and anxious to see the negroes, like the Indians and all other effete and dingy-hued races, gradually exterminated from the face of the whole earth."

Such evil concepts like these do not deserve to be reprinted except to point out that one flash of boldness does not a hero make and that Hinton Helper was a complex mix of ideas, many extremely distasteful. He strove to maintain a career in writing, but his ideas lacked moral validity.

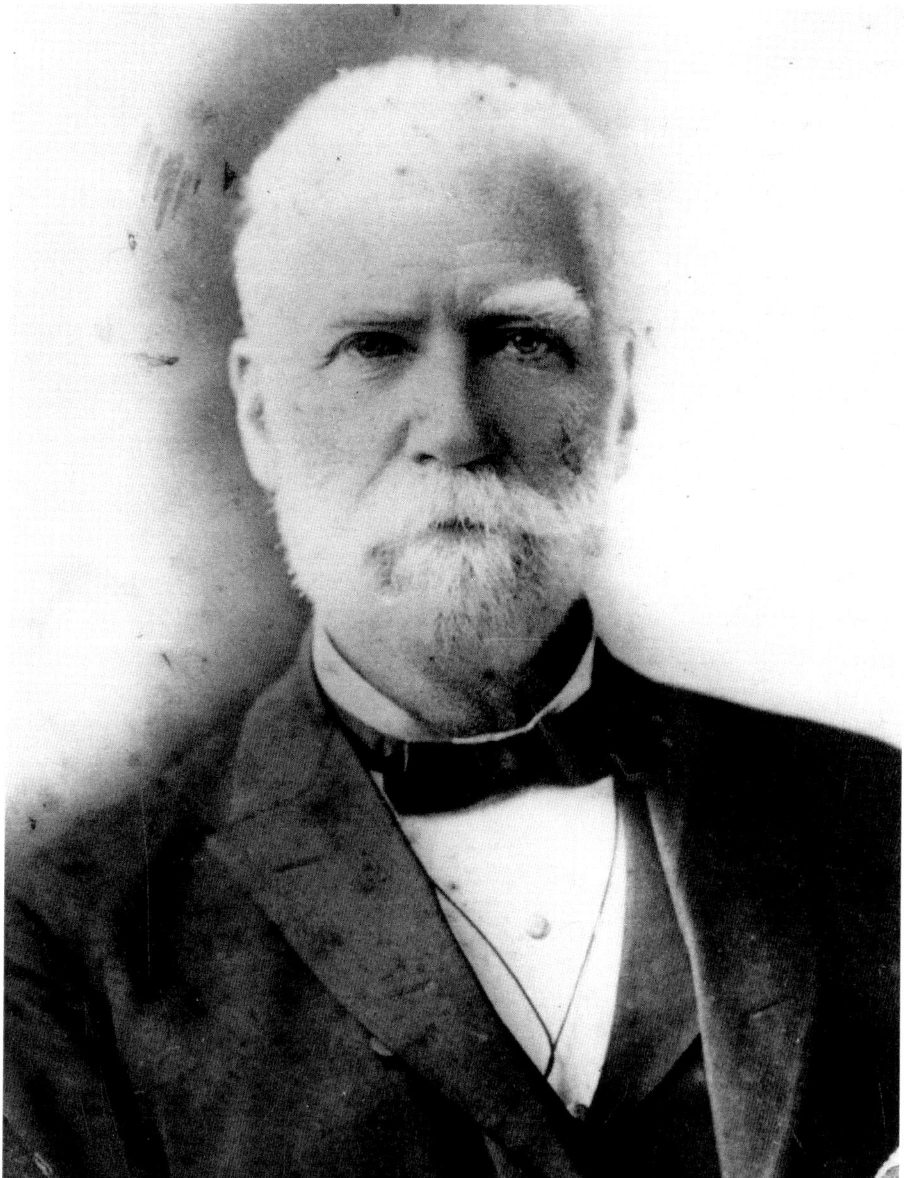

Hinton Helper toward the end of his life. *Collection of the Davie County Public Library.*

Hinton's last years were very sad. His wife went blind and then left him and took their son and only child back to Argentina (where any link of a descendant of Helper's has disappeared in history). Furthermore, his numerous business ventures failed. While he had written of economics in his groundbreaking antislavery book, he was a poor businessman. His biggest undertaking was the plan for a railroad that would run from the southernmost tip of South America through all of that continent and Central America, coursing northward through the United States into Canada. Helper's intention was that the Three Americas Railway would connect the Bering Sea to the Straits of Magellan. He may have grown up on a farm, but he visualized the movement of goods on a large scale during the Industrial Revolution. Sadly, not enough investors shared his vision. He died alone and in poverty. In depression, he took his own life by turning on the gas (utilizing a relatively modern means of suicide) in 1909 in a hotel room, under an assumed name, in Washington, D.C. (he also owned no land at the time of his death). He had perhaps unwittingly traded his North Carolina roots and ties for popularity in the nation's capital years before, and that was where his lonely road in life ended. The newspaper the *Washington Star* reported his last known words to be "There is no justice in this world."

He was buried in what remains today an unmarked grave, uncertain even in its location. The Authors Society paid for a burial place in Forest Lake Cemetery in Maryland, now called Cedar Hill Cemetery, where incidentally African Americans could not be buried until after the civil rights movement of the 1960s. Money never came in (rather a theme in his death as well as his life) for a tombstone, and records indicating exactly where he was buried have been lost to time. Not even a tombstone was ever erected. He did have a World War II U.S. naval ship named in his honor, so his namesake sailed around the world, fitting for a man with a larger world perspective but very different from the railway he envisioned being his legacy. The historical marker on Highway 64 outside Mocksville in rural Davie County that stands in front of the log house in which he was born is his only memorial.

Like Boone, Helper's contribution to history was greatest outside his home state but much more short-lived or recognized than his predecessor. However, the classic work *North Carolina: The History of a Southern State* written by Hugh Lefler, himself a native of Cooleemee in Davie County, makes only a passing mention of Boone but devotes several pages to Helper's book and ideas. Helper stirred the country's passion and his native state's anger over the issue of slavery but struggled to have his book recognized for its detailed work and fought the remainder of his life to find his place. His life began small, escalated to the national stage and then receded just as quickly. Unlike Boone, he peaked by the time he was thirty by writing the right book at the right time in the nation's political passage but never maintained that place in history. He reflected the conflicted times in which he lived and witnessed great surging changes in the nineteenth century but died in the twentieth feeling left behind and not belonging anywhere. Yet while his remains are still lost and no descendants can be determined conclusively in South America, Hinton Helper belongs forever beside Bear Creek in the highway marker that remembers his troubled life.

## *Chapter 5*

# MYSTERY MAN

In 1823, an outsider named Peter Stuart Ney arrived in Mocksville. With a distinctive accent, he introduced himself as a French refugee from the Napoleonic Wars and explained that he was looking for a teaching position. He could not have been more of an outsider, yet he influenced a generation of young boys, including Hinton Helper, in his classroom in rural Davie County.

An observer of Ney's arrival in the area later told the story of Ney interrupting a fight where one man was about to kill another over an insult. Ney challenged the attacker about the fairness of shooting an unarmed man. Rebuked, the aggressor lowered his weapon, and he and Ney became friends. The crowd immediately begged Ney to stay and teach their children. It was later discovered that he had landed in Charleston alone and spent some time in South Carolina before traveling north into more isolated, remote places for a reason.

Peter Ney stayed around and taught in Mocksville for nearly a quarter of a century. (Ironically, this outsider lived much more of his adult life in Mocksville than any of the three young men from Bear Creek storied in this book did.) Students in his classroom remembered one day in particular when a newspaper announcing the death of Napoleon's son landed on his desk. Ney went crazy with grief for days and burned many personal papers. Was it because his dream and last hope of returning to his homeland had died also?

He occasionally talked about his previous life (reportedly most frequently when he had drunk too much) and said that he had hoped to return to France after Napoleon was enthroned. His story was that he was actually Marshal Michel Ney, Napoleon's famous cavalry commander in the Napoleonic Wars, who Napoleon himself had called the "bravest of the brave." All historic accounts state that Marshal Ney was arrested after the Battle of Waterloo, tried for treason and executed by firing squad on December 7, 1815, but bystanders stated that the traditional shot to the head to put the executed out of his misery was not done and his body was not examined before being whisked away. Rumors persisted that his own troops, to whom he gave the command to shoot, had found a way to help him escape after firing over his head. He left behind a wife and sons and with his loyalty to France intact. Was this the same man who emerged in Mocksville eight years later under the name of Peter Ney?

The French Revolution had followed the American Revolutionary War's example, but without the history of self-government that the American colonists had, the French never created a stable new government after overthrowing and executing the royal family. Eventually, a military man named Napoleon became emperor and fought every group of people who had land he believed should be French territory. After his million-man army encountered the Russian winter, he was exiled twice, and twice he returned. Ultimately, he was defeated by the British at the Battle of Waterloo, where his cavalry leader met his fate. Ney was memorialized by a statue in Paris that Ernest Hemingway many years later mentioned in his book *The Sun Also Rises.* He said of it, "He looked very fine, Marshal Ney in his top-boots, gesturing with his sword." That sword is a clue.

Regardless of whether the story of his other life was true or just a good story, Peter Ney somehow quickly won confidence in spite of being a foreigner in a backwoods North Carolina town. He taught in Davie and Iredell County Schools for the next twenty-three years until his death and acquired a reputation as a learned man and gifted teacher, particularly in the many languages he spoke. In addition to being very knowledgeable regarding military matters, he was a skilled equestrian and great at fencing. He also wrote poetry, played the flute and painted, making him considerably more sophisticated than the average backcountry teacher.

His talents were so well known in the area that he was asked to design the seal for Davidson College's first graduation in 1840. He knew the college's first president, Chalmers Davidson, and very likely Hinton's brother "Pink" Helper, also of Davie County, who ran the Helper Hotel in the town of

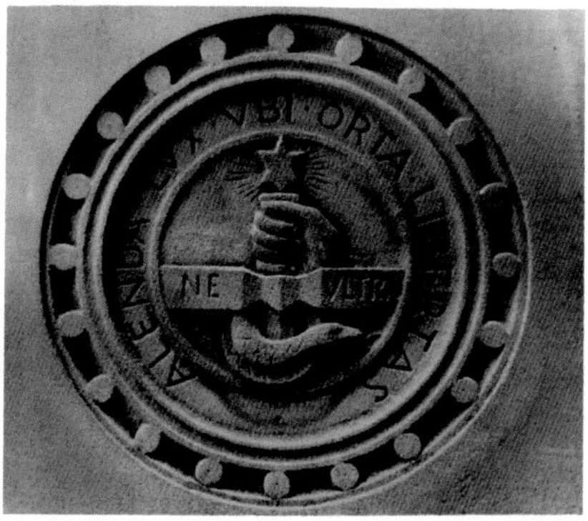

Davidson College seal designed by Peter Ney. *Courtesy of the Archives and Special Collections of Davidson College.*

Davidson. Ney quickly (supposedly during a recess at school) drew the seal that is still used today. It shows a serpent being pierced by a sword held by a strong-looking hand. The most distinctive feature is the diamond on top of the sword that made it resemble a famous similar sword Napoleon had awarded Ney. It had been captured on Ney's person when he was arrested, and allegedly the unusually ornate sword was what gave him away.

One of Ney's Latin textbooks from which he taught is in the holdings of the History Room of the Davie County Public Library. He was a prolific annotator, so his handwriting can be seen throughout the margin notes. At the bottom of one page, he wrote a phrase in Latin with a translation in English, perhaps as a class exercise. The handwriting is hard to make out in a few places, but it begins with a reference to buying a bear hide and ends with the idea of something not being caught. It mirrors a fable by a famous seventeenth-century French writer by the name of Jean de La Fontaine that Ney would have grown up reading. La Fontaine wrote versions of Aesop's Fables with a medieval spin. One such well-known proverb of the time was "Catch the bear before you sell his skin." La Fontaine had written this moral to a story involving two young men who were outsmarted by a bear when trying to obtain its skin that they had promised in exchange for credit at an inn. (The American version of the moral is to not count your chickens before they hatch.) Very likely, Ney told his students this fable, and the North Carolina farm boys in his class could relate to hunting the bear skin. Ney could relate to being the one who got away.

Clues to Peter Ney's true identity include the fact that Peter was the name of Marshal Ney's father, who had fought in the Seven Years' War. Whether or not the son had been inspired as a young red-haired boy, the new teacher often incorporated military practices such as inspecting the students in rank and file order. He spoke of the Napoleonic Wars with a sense of firsthand experience. On several occasions, including on his deathbed, he identified himself as Marshal Ney. He would have been about the correct age also.

Davidson College has in its holdings (along with a lap desk, flute and compass holder that belonged to Ney) a small book on French history

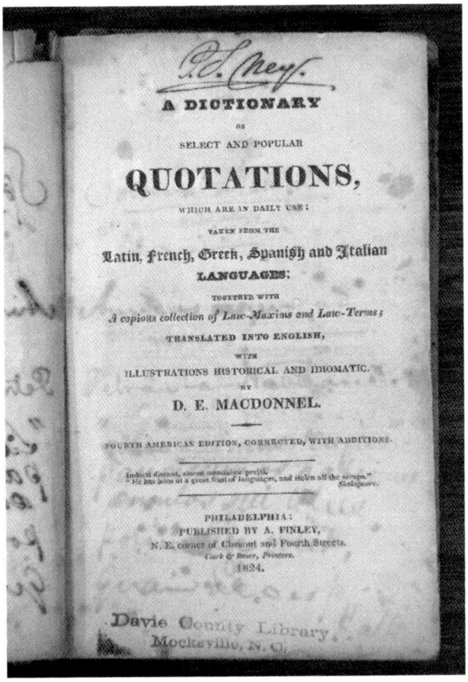


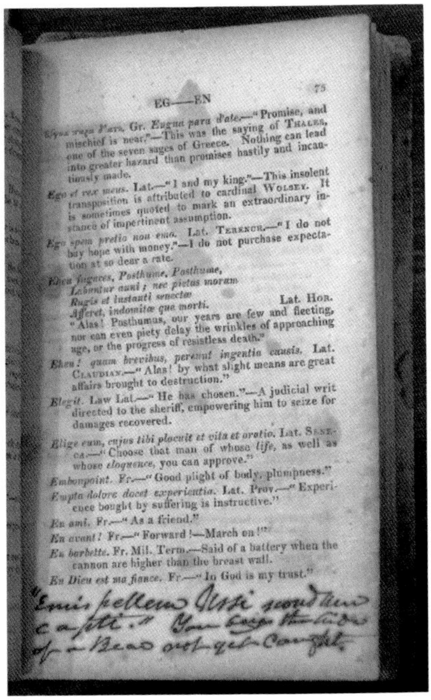


*Left*: Latin textbook Ney used as a teacher. *Collection of the author.*

*Right*: Marginal notes in Latin and English in Ney's textbook. *Collection of the author.*

published during Peter Ney's lifetime. In volume two of *History of Napoleon* written by M. Laurent de L'Ardeche there is a printed drawing of Marshal Ney. On this copy only there appears a pencil sketch of a man's profile that strongly resembles the man in the artwork with the words "Ney by him self" beside it, indicating that local teacher Peter Ney had added this self-portrait in a revelatory moment. Obviously, he could have done that if simply trying to lay claim to the fame. Or it could have been a clue to his real identity.

Many people in history have claimed to be famous deceased people. Most recently, Anna Anderson of Virginia claimed to be Anastasia, the Russian duchess who was the youngest daughter of Nicholas and Alexandria, the last royal rulers in Russia. In 1917, during the Bolshevik Revolution, the royal family was captured and killed, with their graves just being confirmed since the fall of Communism. Anna Anderson surfaced in the United States, about the right age and with personal stories no one could prove or disprove. However, at her death in 1986, DNA tests were compared to Prince Philip

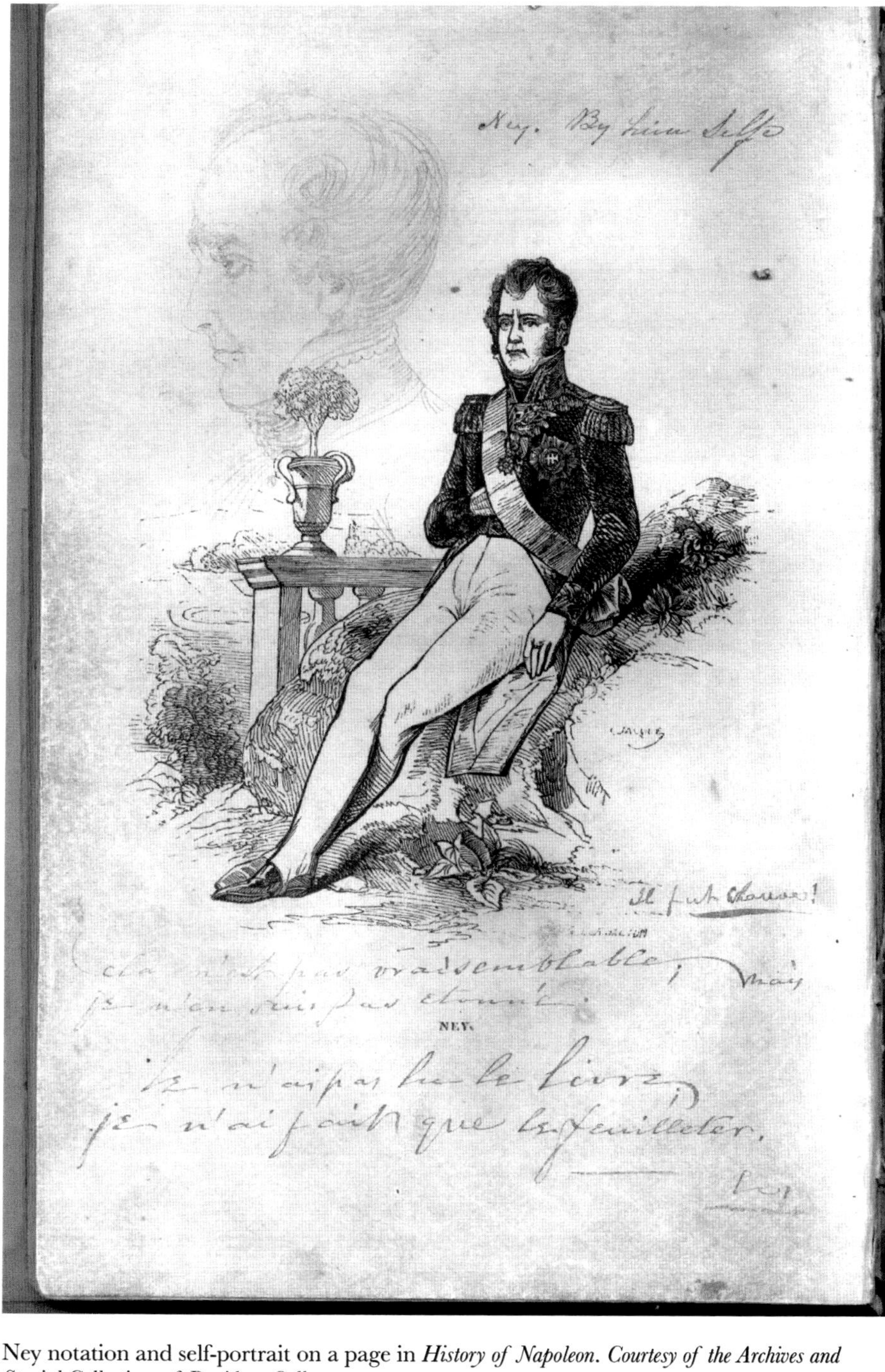


Ney notation and self-portrait on a page in *History of Napoleon. Courtesy of the Archives and Special Collections of Davidson College.*

of England, as they would have both been descendants of Queen Victoria, and the results proved she could not have been the duchess.

Was Peter Ney the same person as Marshal Michel Ney? Sadly, no portrait exists of Peter Ney of Mocksville (other than the sketch in that one book that he most likely drew himself) to compare with the ones of Marshal Ney. All personal impressions of Peter Ney speak of his tall stature, knowledge and mastery of the sword, things consistent with Marshal Ney. Handwriting analysis done in Charlotte decided his and Ney's were a match, but one by the FBI called it inconclusive. Accounts of physical scars could align with Marshall Ney's battle wounds—a bullet in the leg and a saber cut to the head. Furthermore, his lawyers reportedly continued to attempt to get his sentence of death reversed for twenty years after his supposed execution—perhaps so he could return to his beloved France in his lifetime. It was believed he continued to communicate with his wife through lawyers as well. Peter Ney's remains were exhumed twice, in 1887 and 1936, but nothing could be determined. Could it be determined today with modern DNA match testing? That is questionable since Marshal Ney's four sons in France never produced any offspring with whom to compare their DNA for a match. It would be necessary to exhume one of his sons' bodies to

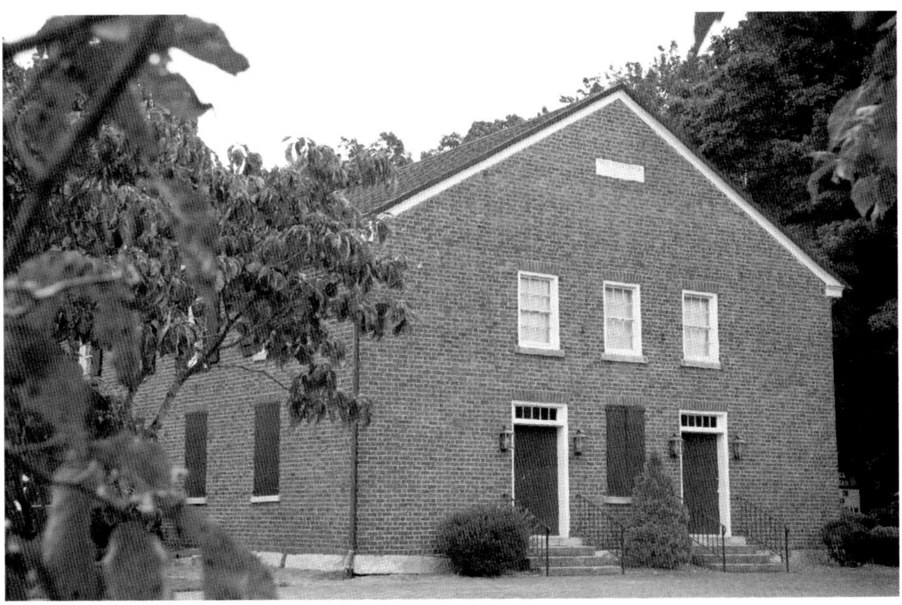

Third Creek Presbyterian Church chapel. *Collection of the author.*

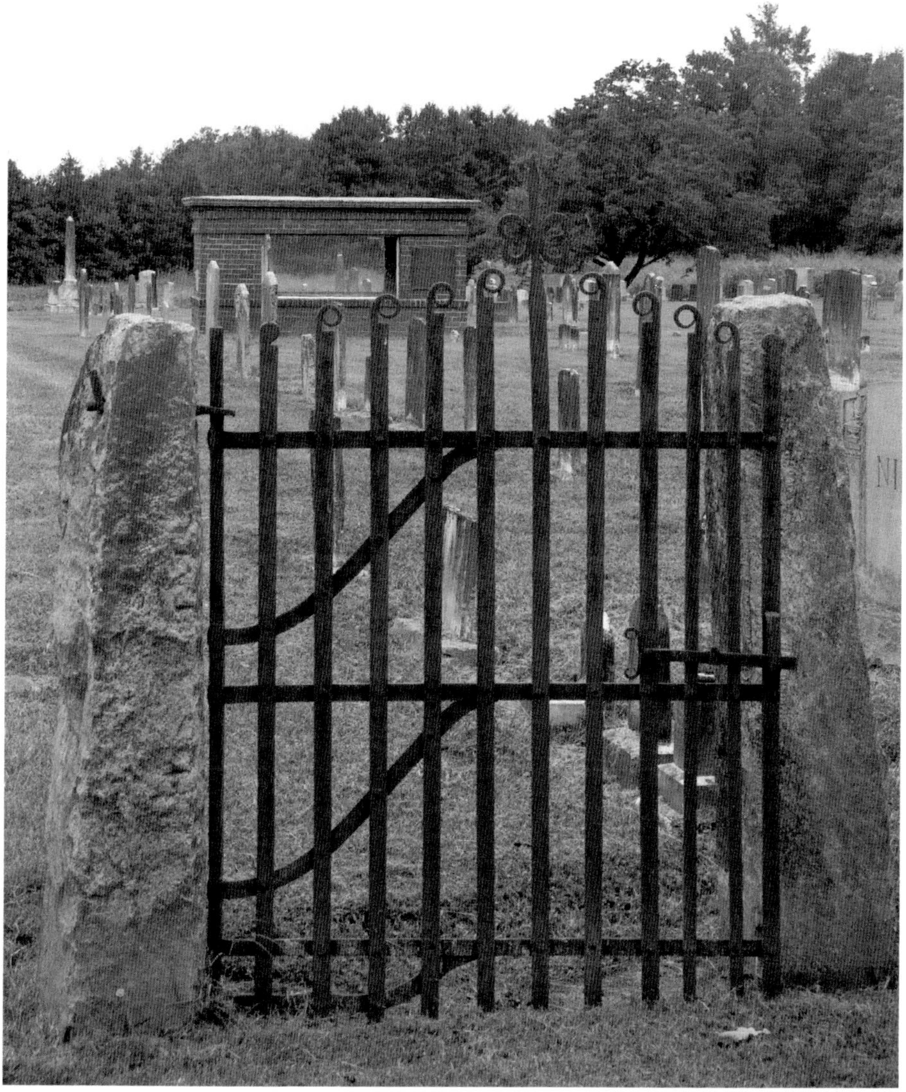

Third Creek Presbyterian Church cemetery, where Peter Ney is buried. *Collection of Stephen Phillips.*

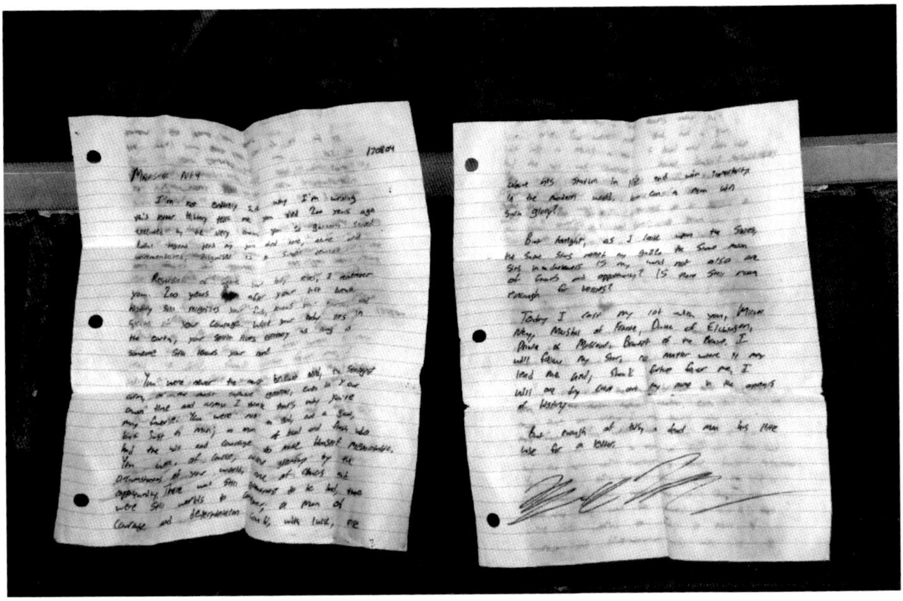

Letter left at Ney's tombstone. *Collection of the author.*

check for a match. It seems odd that a man with four sons would not have any descendants alive today. Exactly the same situation is true of President Abraham Lincoln, who had four sons but after his last great-grandson died in 1985, no direct descendant is alive. Other famous people with no living biological descendants include William Shakespeare, George Washington and Mark Twain.

Peter Stuart Ney's life ended in 1846, far from his homeland of France, just over the line into Rowan County. He had lived his last days with a former student named Osborne Giles Foard, who later was a major railroad builder and legislator in North Carolina. One witness related that on his deathbed, when attending physician and another former student of his Dr. Matthew Locke asked him, Peter Ney stated he was, indeed, Marshal Ney and referred his friends to a written story of his escape, written in French, but that piece of paper disappeared in the hands of a translator. Famous lecturer Pliny Miles took it to New York to be translated, and it vanished from history. Might this piece of history still be hidden somewhere in an archives or someone's attic?

Ney was buried at Third Creek Presbyterian Church in Cleveland (although Ney presumably was a Catholic if he was a Frenchman) among many Scots. His funeral service was held in the newly built sanctuary that still stands. Ney's tombstone, placed by former students of his, reflects his claims and reads, "A native of France and soldier of the French Revolution under Napoleon Bonaparte." But the mystery remains unsolved. Many visitors to his tomb leave tributes, such as stones, pinecones and even a letter tucked into the edge of the glass stating how inspired a young man of the twenty-first century was by Ney's courage.

Whoever Peter Ney was before he landed in North Carolina, from all accounts he was an exceptional teacher who challenged and inspired his students, including Hinton Helper, to greatness. He contributed to the knowledge of a whole generation and introduced them to the greater world. He was not from Davie County, but he became part of the fabric woven here. And unlike the other three men, he lived out his life and died here, but like them, he had left home to never return.

*Chapter 6*

# THOMAS FEREBEE

Nine years after Hinton Helper's death, a baby named Thomas Wilson Ferebee was born in Davie County on November 9, 1918, mere hours before the armistice of World War I (famously at the eleventh hour on the eleventh day of the eleventh month). World War I had been declared to be the war that would end all wars, but it was merely a rehearsal for the greater conflict that followed two decades later. By the time World War II was closing, that baby would have participated in a key event on the other side of the world. Ironically, a child born in the waning hours of the first worldwide conflict would nearly twenty-seven years later help define the end of the second. All that would have seemed inconceivable to the farm family in which Thomas was the third born of eventually eleven children.

While his family moved fifteen times, much of Tom Ferebee's youth was spent living on Angell Road in the community of Cana. Even a century ago, Cana was just a group of homes clustered near a store/post office and a school. Cana had played a brief role in the Civil War that Hinton Helper helped initiate when Stoneman's Raid crashed through the community on its way to meet General Sherman's movement north. Today, Cana is just a concentration of farms with a deep, lingering sense of community.

Thomas was born to parents who lived their entire lives in Davie County. His mother, Zella Ward, was of Dutch descent and from the community of Farmington. The Ferebee side of the family was British and had been among the earliest settlers in the area, along with the Boones, so the family had deep roots in Davie County by the time Thomas was born. But that

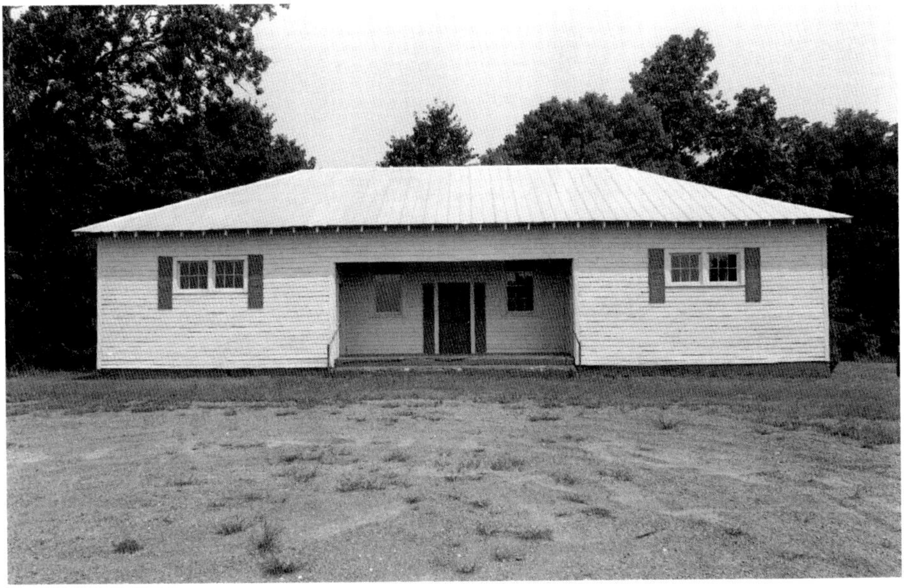

A twentieth-century photograph of Cana School. *Collection of the Davie County Public Library.*

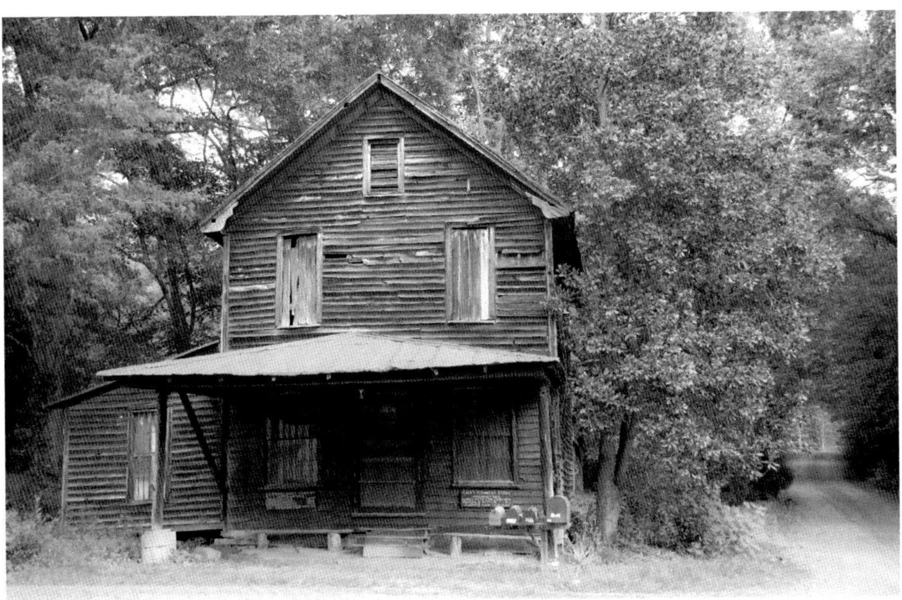

Cana historic post office/store, still standing. *Collection of Stephen Phillips.*

time had not brought the family to wealth or prominence, and his parents moved repeatedly to rented farms in an economic arrangement called tenant farming. The family did not own its own land until it bought 150 acres in 1940 on Highway 64 near Bear Creek.

Thomas's father, William "Flav," was the typical head of a large farming family where everyone contributed labor and struggled to maintain a hardscrabble existence. Thomas became a teenager just as the Great Depression settled in for a long, hard stretch. However, for a family already living at a subsistence level, the Depression did not depress their lives as much as others with investments at risk. They were able to feed themselves from their gardens, and not owning their own home and land meant they could stay on a farm that was not theirs to lose. Tenant farming most often was based on a system where rent was paid with a portion of the crop produced, most commonly cotton and tobacco in this area, so cash flow was not as significant. Survivors of that generation often said, "The Depression came and went and we never knew it," because a farm family's life was not as severely impacted as they lived off the land. Tom's younger brother Bill (who remained an avid hunter all his life in Davie County) recalled how often their dad took his sons fishing in nearby creeks, for sport but also probably for a good supper of pan-fried fish. Furthermore, education was free, as were simple pastimes like sandlot baseball and porch sitting.

As Tom participated in local life, he was given opportunities like a trip to Washington, D.C., as a group of agricultural students when he was a senior in high school. On this occasion, he got his picture in the local newspaper for the first time. He also participated in sports, particularly excelling at baseball and football, and was known to walk miles to the high school in Mocksville in the snow with his brother Bill to play ball. Unfortunately, a football knee injury would later end any chances of a career in sports and alter his dreams of a career in aviation.

The relatively new invention of flight caught Tom's imagination. He read about Charles Lindbergh's flight when he was about ten years old and spent much time looking up at airplanes after that, including one time when he was caught out of bed when sick with the measles. He also paid hard-earned money for a joyride with a barnstorming pilot when he was a teen.

North Carolina had already claimed a place in aviation history. Orville and Wilbur Wright built their flyer in the back of their bicycle shop in Dayton, Ohio, but the first time it flew off the earth, that ground below it was North Carolina sand. Only fifteen years before Ferebee was born, man soared above the earth in a powered machine for the first time over Kitty Hawk

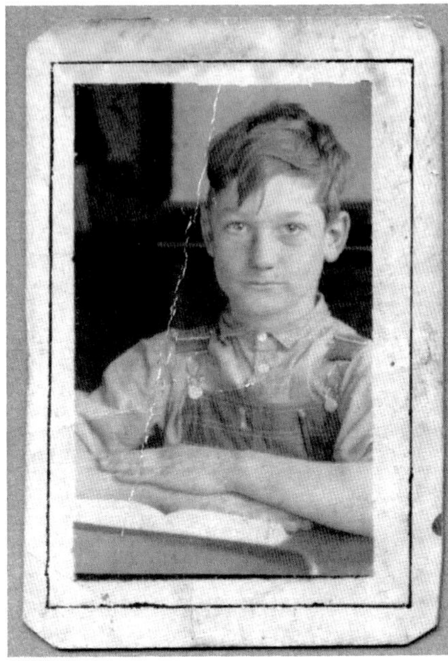

School picture of Tom Ferebee. *Collection of North Carolina Museum of History.*

in the Outer Banks. The brothers chose the place to test their flights for a very important reason: sand dunes provided a soft landing for what was a very risky experiment. They had repeatedly shipped their flyers in parts by train from Ohio to North Carolina. On December 17, 1903, in their last try before returning home for Christmas, the brothers took turns in the plane behind the controls until successfully flying for just fifty-nine seconds ten feet above the ground (the flyer hangs twice as high above the floor of the Smithsonian today as it ever flew above the ground). The Wright brothers were such a team that most people cannot even name which one was the first man to fly a plane—it was Orville. After trial attempts in many places, it was North Carolina that first witnessed flight, and a few years later, a small North Carolina boy named Tom gazed in the sky at planes overhead long before he gazed down upon the earth from one.

Ferebee's favorite youthful pastime, however, was hunting, particularly rabbits and raccoons, both animals still found in abundance in rural Davie County and still actively hunted. Thomas was later given the nickname "Coon Ferebee" by his military buddies as a result of his telling so many hunting stories in that distinctive Davie County cadence (it was said that he never lost his country drawl). One of the things his buddies in the military most recalled about him was that he loved to hunt. No doubt like so many local hunters, he roamed far and wide in the patches of woods common in the area but had favorite spots as well. He may well have hunted the same woods and fields that Daniel Boone had so many years before him and possibly, unknowingly to each other, shared the same favorite spots. Unlike Boone, Tom's hunting was for fun and food rather than for trade and income.

Tom was voted most athletic in his 1940 high school yearbook, and sports made it possible for him to attend college on an athletic scholarship to Lees-McRae College in Banner Elk. He and a cousin earned extra funds for college by laying power lines into the mountains, bringing the benefit of electricity to the remote hills for the first time. The college could not afford a baseball team, so he played football and basketball and ran track but left college to try out for a St. Louis Cardinals farm team. He dreamed of being the catcher but did not make the cut and left disappointed that he had not been ready for his big chance. He returned to college to finish his two-year degree and planned to go on to Davidson College, which did have a baseball team. He spent the summer practicing his pitch and played with the R.J. Reynolds Tobacco Company team.

It was while he was at college that his family relocated to a farm on U.S. Highway 64, still known then as the road to Statesville. It was the fifteenth home the family had lived in over the previous twenty-five years, but this one was different because they were able to buy it for $7,000 with the help of a government loan. So Tom spent the school break at home that summer, no doubt throwing baseballs at the barn or some other target but also exploring and hunting the same area around Bear Creek that Boone had 160 years earlier and where Helper had played a century before.

During that summer of 1940, Tom gave a lot of thought to the escalating war in Europe. It seemed inevitable that the United States would be drawn into the war, and he was the perfect age to be drafted. His love of aviation prompted him to take action that would give him an advantage over just being a foot soldier. He made a tough decision, and one about which he later expressed regret, to not continue at Davidson College or pursue a career in baseball. Instead, Tom applied for the U.S. Army Air Corps Aviation Cadet Program and was accepted. On September 16, 1941, he left Mocksville on a bus bound for Charlotte, heading for Hicks Field near Fort Worth, Texas, where the course of his life changed.

World War I was first called the Great War due to its global span. It would not be called the first such war until there was a second, and many believe the way Germany was punished by the victors after the first war gave rise to the second only twenty years later. America had stepped into the Great War only to help the Allies the last year, after which it returned to its historic position of remaining isolated from European troubles. That all changed when Europe went to war after Adolf Hitler invaded Poland on September 1, 1939. The American magazine *TIME* first called the conflict World War II in its September 11 (ironically) issue. Americans watched their distant relatives fight on another continent and found it harder to feel neutral. The United States officially remained uninvolved, but after Japan attacked the American naval post of Pearl Harbor in Hawaii on December 7, 1941, Americans joined World War II.

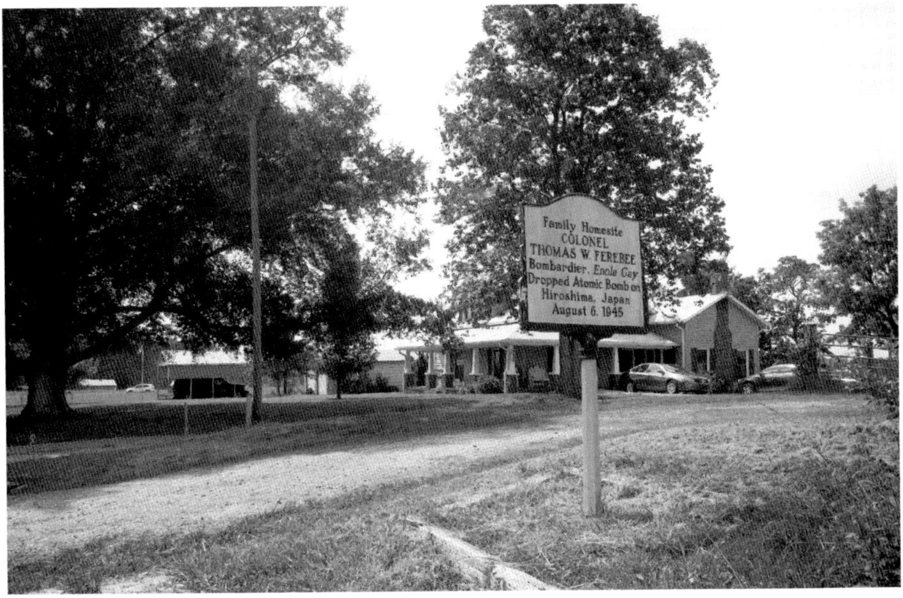


Ferebee historic marker and farmhouse on U.S. Highway 64. *Collection of the author.*

Meanwhile, Tom's dreams of flying were derailed by several challenges: the old football knee injury made it difficult for him to handle the rudder pedals in the BT-14 plane, and he was criticized in training for being too "hot-dogger" and daring in maneuvers. Risk taking does not always guarantee success. He left and returned to Mocksville, disappointed again. He spent another summer playing ball locally, hunting, fishing and thinking on his future. By the end of the summer, he had applied to train with a new program, the U.S. Army Air Forces Bombardier Training. He was rejected at first due to his poor performance in the aviation program but persisted with pleading letters sent to leaders in Washington, D.C., and was finally accepted. The army was quickly escalating its ability to bomb targets, and Tom happened upon the chance at just the right time. Timing was everything. By October, he was on his way to Maxwell Air Field in Alabama and ultimately to history.

The boy who wanted to play baseball in the big leagues or fly an airplane failed at both, but at least he knew his chances of surviving World War II were questionable and discovered another second route to a meaningful life. Tom's brother Bill Ferebee also served during the war in the U.S. Navy, in the South Pacific, where he was a turret gunner and B-26 plane crew chief, rising to the rank of captain. When it came to defending the homeland, the

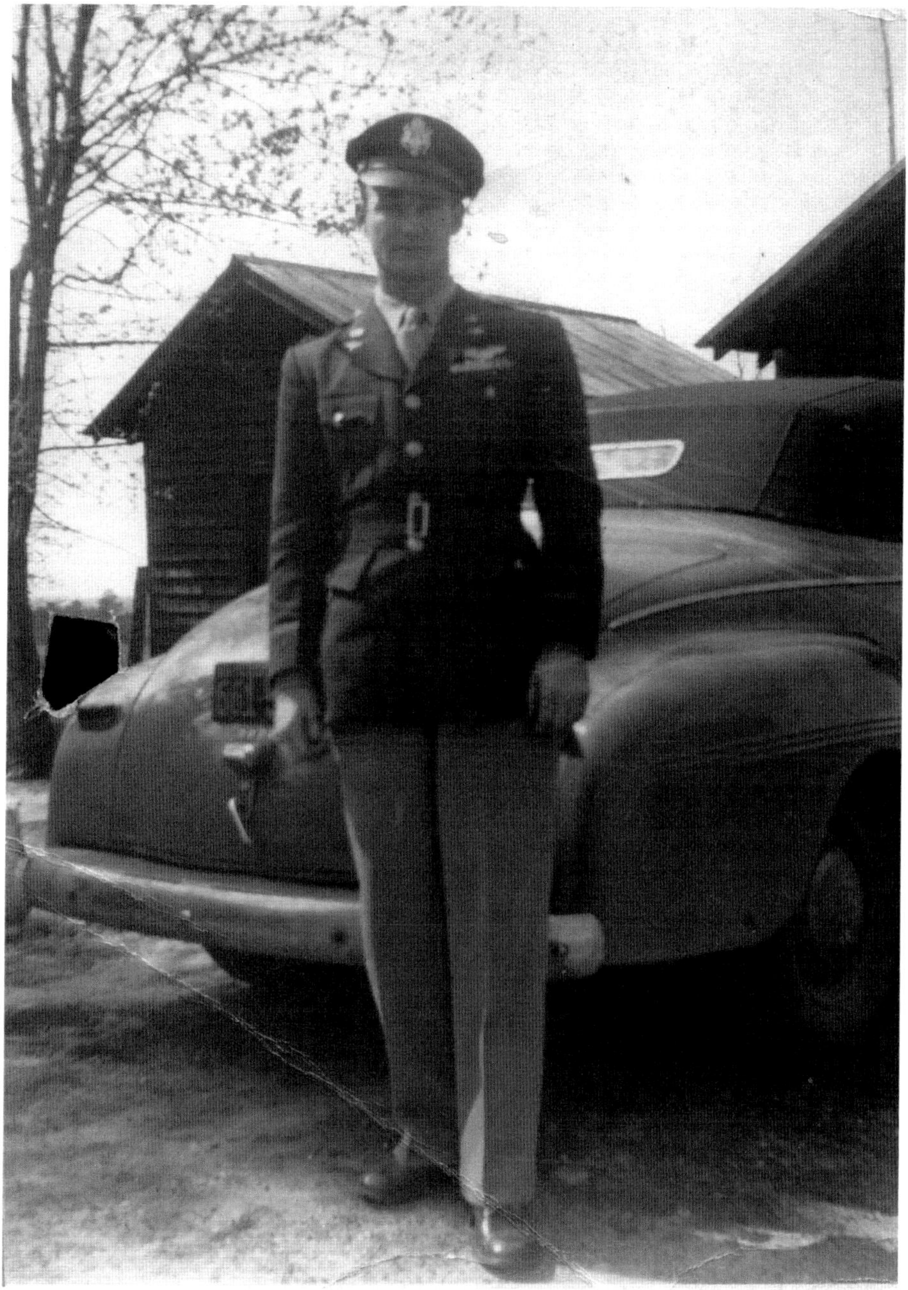

Tom Ferebee on military leave at his family farm. *Collection of North Carolina Museum of History.*

Ferebee family was all in. A book with the title *The Three Musketeers of the Army Air Forces* by Robert O. Harper tells the story of Tom Ferebee's military career and those of two other men so crucial to the *Enola Gay*'s role in history.

Tom excelled at the precision necessary for target bombing, perhaps because of his experience pitching a baseball and sighting on a hunting gun, and was soon stationed at Sarasota Army Air Field in Florida. There he learned that the program was so new that many of his superiors had little more experience than he did. They were flying the B-17, the later famous "Flying Fortress" of the war. The Flying Fortress dropped more bombs in World War II than any other United States aircraft. It was fast and could fly at high altitudes and over long distances. In addition, it had a high record of being able to return safely even if damaged by gunfire. Tom Ferebee would drop bombs on sixty-five missions over North Africa and Europe, many of them from this formidable aircraft and many times on the city of Ploesti, Romania, which was a major oil refinery for the Nazi military efforts. Destroying the fuel supply made this mission critical to the war effort.

Tom graduated from the training program in March 1942 and was made a second lieutenant. In Sarasota, he met a navigator named Ted Van Kirk and a pilot named Paul Tibbets. They would become lifelong friends and together made history a few years later. As Tom perfected his skills to hit a target far below him, he got better and better and was promoted to captain and then major. Along the way, he led the first bombing on Nazi-occupied France and was the lead bombardier in the first one-hundred-plane bombing raid in which the United States participated.

The term "bombardier" has as its root the word "bombard," which has historically meant to attack relentlessly until the enemy surrenders. While the military preferred the term "bomb aimer," "bombardier" is the term that persisted until later in the twentieth century when a computer replaced the person. As a bombardier, Tom would learn to load and position a bomb and then pick the exact best moment to release it with a "bombs away!"

His biggest target was soon to come into sight, but he would spend nearly a year training for the mission of a lifetime. He was handpicked by Colonel Tibbets, who called him "the best bombardier who ever looked through the eyepiece of a Norden." The Norden was a bombsighting device that offered remarkable accuracy in hitting a target. It was so top secret that it was removed from the plane when it was on the ground, and the crew was sworn to protect it with their lives if necessary. Nevertheless, Tom had a string of misses during bombing practice. Tibbets noticed that Tom would raise himself up at the last minute for a visual image of the target, and that

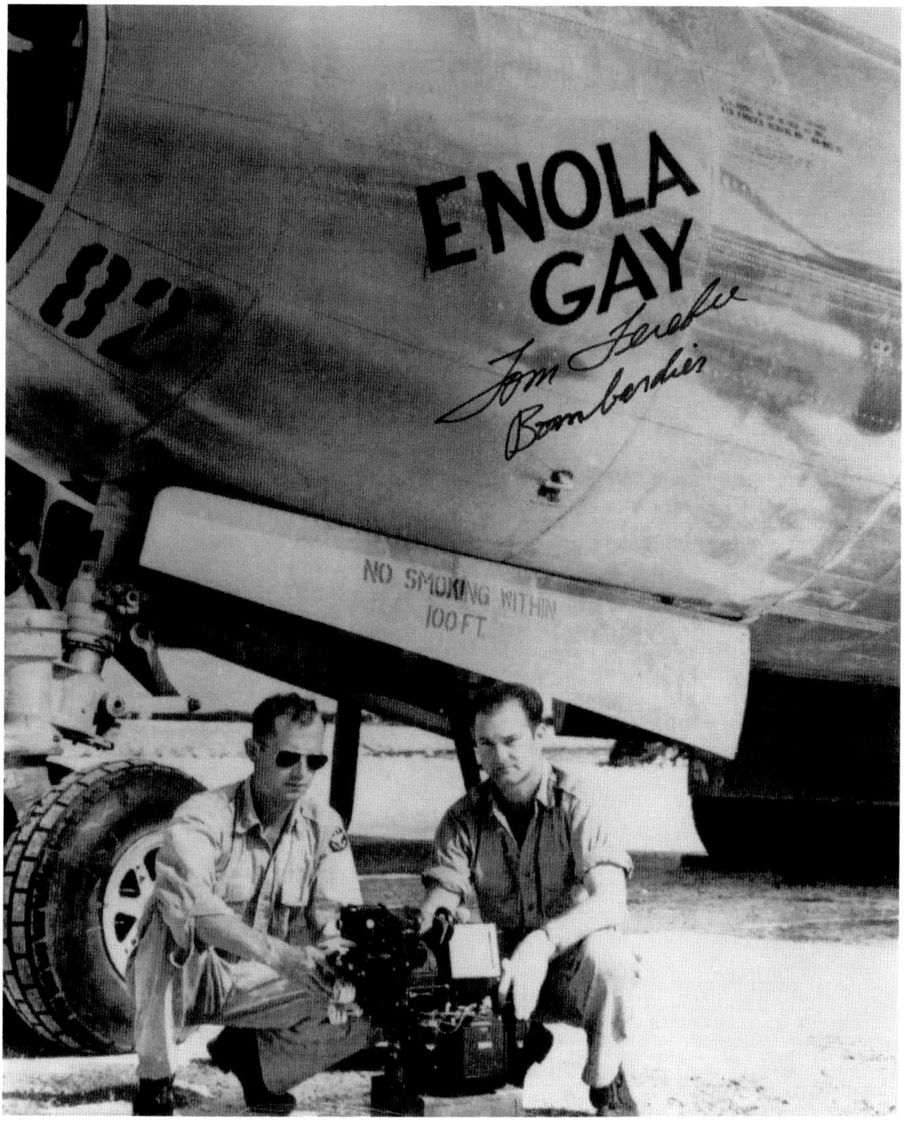


A Thomas Ferebee autographed photograph of him and Van Kirk with the Norden device. *Collection of the author.*

threw off his delivery. Tibbets made a head rest for him, and that solved the problem by ensuring he would remain still.

The development of a weapon that would use nuclear fission had been in the works since 1939, when Europe was already at war but the United

States was not yet. Called the Manhattan Project, it was so secretive that President Harry S Truman, who would order its use, did not know of its existence until months before. The work was mostly carried out in a remote rural location, Oak Ridge, Tennessee. The town was taken over by the U.S. government and became primarily a disguise for what was happening out of sight. Security was so tight around the town that apparently the coffins of local residents had to be opened and checked before burial.

In the summer of 1945, the team of Tibbets, Van Kirk and Ferebee was summoned to a very secretive project and location in the Mariana Islands in the Pacific Ocean, where a special new atomic bomb, referred to as Little Boy (ironic since Little Boy weighed nine thousand pounds), was being prepared for use. While the logistics were being worked out, a smaller version of the bomb was tested successfully in the desert of New Mexico. While waiting to hear the results, the men in a remote location, an island in the South Seas, often played softball to pass the time. Tom Ferebee was the catcher, playing ball in a very different game than he had imagined—one of waiting for orders.

"Little Boy" was an interesting and innocent-sounding codename for the world's most powerful weapon ever devised. It was very different from a little boy gazing up in the sky in Davie County, and yet it was in the hands of someone who had been just that. The little boy who had looked to the skies would now look down from the skies on the largest target ever, and everything he had learned as a little boy went into guiding the soon-to-be-famous one.

The B-29 plane that would carry the Little Boy was also especially designed for this mission. Albert Einstein, in a letter to President Franklin Roosevelt in 1939, had proposed the possibility of an atomic fission bomb but expressed the opinion that any such bomb would be much too heavy to be transported by an airplane. The solution was to reconfigure the Superfortress with a technique called silverplating to lighten the weight of the plane by thousands of pounds by substituting fuel injection engines and removing armor plate. A bonus was these lighter planes could fly higher than any fighter planes or antiaircraft fire could reach. An extremely secretive military unit was formed, called the 509$^{th}$ Composite Group, under the leadership of Colonel Paul Tibbets with the responsibility of delivering one special weapon.

The assembly of the Little Boy was completed in a South Pacific hut on July 30, 1945. Only two days before, a military plane, a B-25 Mitchell, had crashed into the Empire State Building in New York City. The pilot and two others on the plane had lost all visibility due to thick fog and flew directly into the seventy-ninth floor of the tallest building then in the world (it would not be surpassed until 1972 by the World Trade Center Twin Towers). Mirroring the events of September 11, 2001, in so many ways, a nation still at war with Japan (the war with Europe had ended May 7) immediately thought the nation's largest city was under attack, and panic ensued. The force of the plane sent its parts propelling through the other side of the building and raining down on the streets as the fuel tanks exploded. Fortunately, it was a Saturday and the building was mostly empty. Only eleven people in the building were killed, ironically all employees of a War Relief Services office. The gaping, fiery hole turned all eyes toward it and highlighted the damage a plane could do. The building was structurally sound and rebuilt quickly, but the fear was real and lasting. It is uncertain when news of this disaster reached the men in training on the small island on the other side of the world, but no doubt they pondered the disaster they were commissioned to create and the fear it would generate. Their mission was only a week away. Ironically, any newspaper pictures of the Empire State Building after this event would have looked strangely familiar to Thomas Ferebee, who had played for the R.J. Reynolds ball team in neighboring Winston-Salem. The Reynolds Building in Winston-Salem, North Carolina, was built in 1929 as the tobacco company's corporate headquarters. At the time, at twenty-one floors, it was the tallest building in the South and served as a model for and was a miniature version of the Empire State Building, built two years later in New York City. To this day, every Father's Day, the staff at the Empire State Building sends a Father's Day card to the staff at the Reynolds Building in Winston-Salem.

President Harry S Truman had already approved the use of Little Boy at any time after he returned from the Potsdam Conference on August 2. All that was needed and waited on in the end was a day with the right weather in the sky, a geographical factor that could not be ignored or controlled. No instruments could substitute for a good visual. The Empire State Building crash in New York City proved that. After a week of clouds over Japan, the skies were finally clear on the morning of August 6, 1945.

On that bright, clear morning, Tom Ferebee found himself flying on the *Enola Gay* with pilot Colonel Paul Tibbets and Captain Ted Van Kirk, who went by the nickname "Dutch." There had been many last-minute preparations and a few hurdles. Dutch had actually been hospitalized briefly for a bad case of hives, either caused by a reaction to local tomatoes or nerves. And Colonel Tibbets had his own special mission—he asked that the lead plane, a B-29 that implemented new turbojet technology, be given

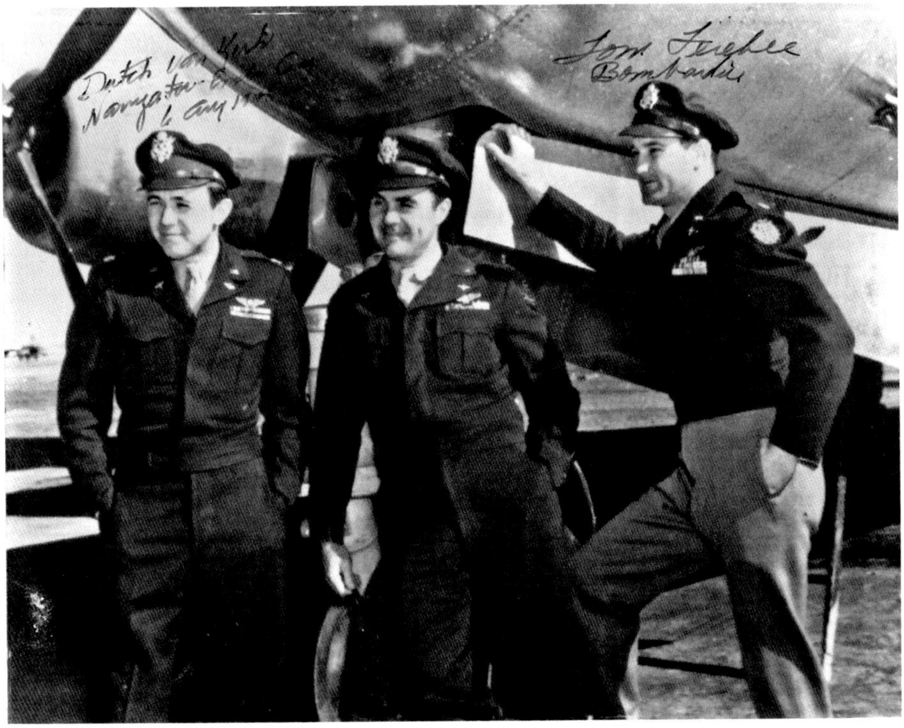


*Enola Gay* crew of Ferebee, Tibbets and Van Kirk. *Collection of the Davie County Public Library.*

the name of his mother, who had inspired and supported him in becoming a pilot. The team agreed, and it was christened the *Enola Gay*. The night before, twenty-five-year-old chaplain Pastor William Downey of Hope Lutheran Church in Minneapolis had led the somber group in prayer.

The mission actually was a formation of three planes. The flight from the island of Tinian to their Japanese target of Hiroshima took thirteen hours, and Ferebee was so calm he slept much of the way, including through Tibbets's explanation to the rest of the crew the nature of this unique mission and the significance of the weapon they were carrying. No matter—Ferebee already knew. There was no reason to question it, and he knew the significance and danger. There was only one bomb on the plane.

Hiroshima was chosen because it had not been bombed in other raids, because it was the right size and because it was a concentrated location of military troops and weapons. The planes arrived over Hiroshima a little after 8:00 a.m. local time, when most residents had just started their work or school day. Thirty-two thousand feet above them, the focus was on different matters. Tom Ferebee of Davie County did not have the weight of the decision to make; it had already been made, and he had simply one job to do. When the right moment came, Tom carefully positioned the bomb into the correct angle to drop it, all the while visually spotting the city, with the Ota River coursing through it, in his own words, "like the fingers of a hand." He sighted in on the Aioi Bridge, stating later that it was a fairly easy target to hit. With the verbal instructions of location, he pulled the manual release handle with his right hand and then seconds later pulled the emergency release handle with his left hand so hard he almost wrenched it loose. He correctly stated the singular nature of this weapon with a "Bomb away!" He then peered out at the bomb, Little Boy, surging toward its target, as was his practice, until forty-five seconds later a tremendous beam of light almost blinded him. He and Tibbets were both temporarily blinded, as they had failed to put on the protective goggles prepared for them, but not before he witnessed the following, recorded in an interview with the *Charlotte Observer*: "At first, I saw this boiling on the ground and the stem [of the mushroom cloud] was going up and you could see buildings going up in the stem." He realized he had flattened a city. The next day, his parents learned that Tom had been involved when a reporter called them. They voiced that they were proud of him and relieved he was not hurt. Davie County's native son had delivered.

Tail gunner Bob Caron was the only person on the *Enola Gay* or otherwise to capture on film the mushroom cloud that ascended from the explosion at Hiroshima. (Other photos are often attributed to this event, even in museums, but they depict Nagasaki or test explosions.) This picture was distributed on thousands of flyers dropped over Nagasaki as warning the very next day.

Three days later, another atomic bomb was dropped over Nagasaki, and that brought the Japanese to surrender. These drastic measures had produced the desired success and victory. While dropping the first atomic bomb in history had been a massive team effort, it was the precision and expertise of the bombardier, the Davie County farm boy, whose hunting skills allowed him to hit his target that ensured the end of the greatest war in history.

The United States' relationship with the nation of Japan was at its lowest, but as a generous victor, the American government worked hard to rebuild the defeated country, sending everything from engineers to businessmen to missionaries and millions of dollars. The relationship healed, and Japan has become one of America's best allies. Evidence of this is that one of

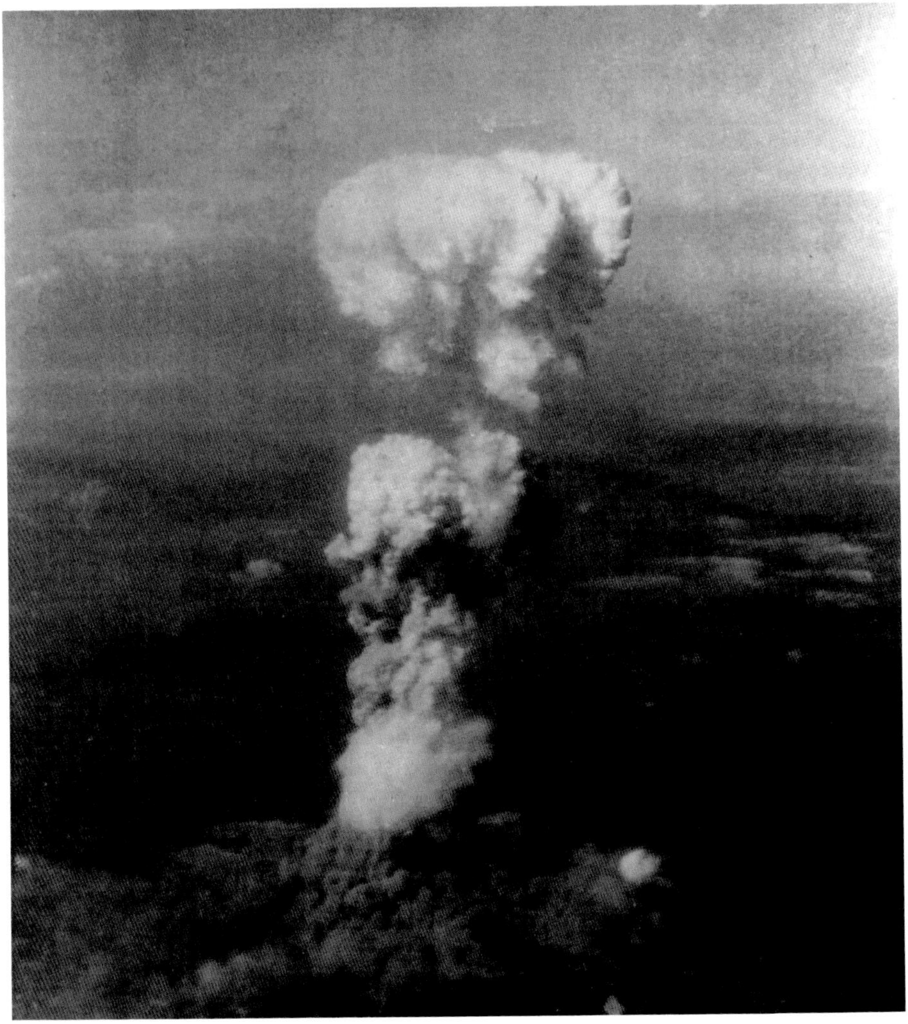

Bob Caron's photograph of the mushroom cloud after the Hiroshima bombing. *Collection of the National Archives.*

the sailors who captained the PT 109 boat sunk by a Japanese destroyer in the Pacific during World War II became President John F. Kennedy, whose daughter Caroline Kennedy was the ambassador to Japan at the time of the fiftieth anniversary of the Hiroshima bombing.

Remembering his important role years later, Thomas Ferebee expressed no regrets for the bombing, just the lives lost. "I'm sorry an awful lot of people died from that bomb, and I hate to think that something like that had to happen to end the war," he said in the *Charlotte Observer* interview on the fiftieth anniversary of the bombing. "People have to go back and study the history of the war and the attitude of the people at that time," he said. "Everybody wanted the war to end. That's what I wanted the most. I wanted the bomb to work and end the war." When a local man asked him the question everyone asked him, Thomas Ferebee answered the same every time: "I would do it again. I never lost a moment of sleep over it."

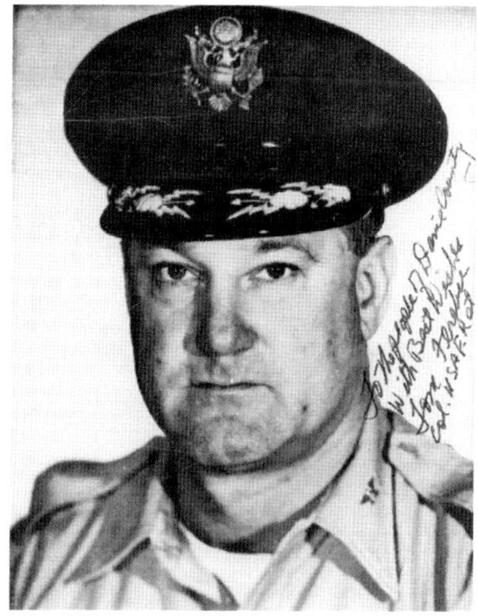

Thomas Ferebee signed picture expressing his appreciation for Davie County. *Collection of the Davie County Public Library.*

Following the war, the *Enola Gay* was virtually abandoned at an airfield and in storage for almost fifty years before being restored and displayed at the Smithsonian Museum. Feelings toward the bombing were so mixed that it made the plane itself controversial.

Thomas was only twenty-six years old when he participated in the bombing of Hiroshima. The defining moment of his life had happened before he even turned thirty. He would remain in the army until 1970 and served during both Vietnam and the Cold War conflicts and even a stint stationed with NATO before he retired from the military with the rank of colonel and went into the real estate business in Florida. He not only owned land at his death but had made sure many others did also. He, Tibbets and Van Kirk remained close friends for the rest of their lives and appeared together in Mocksville on May 27, 1991, when the war monument in the downtown square was dedicated.

Thomas Ferebee died in retirement in Florida in the year 2000, at the beginning of another new century in American history. His hometown of Mocksville gave him a hero's farewell, the only one of its local boys accorded that and the only one to be buried back in Davie County. A bridge was named for him on Highway 64 that crosses Bear Creek. He was buried with his family in the Wesley Chapel Methodist Church cemetery with a simple military tombstone, with his flying companions and close friends Paul Tibbets and Dutch Van Kirk at the funeral. The skies over Mocksville saw a flyover honoring his burial as elderly veterans stood at

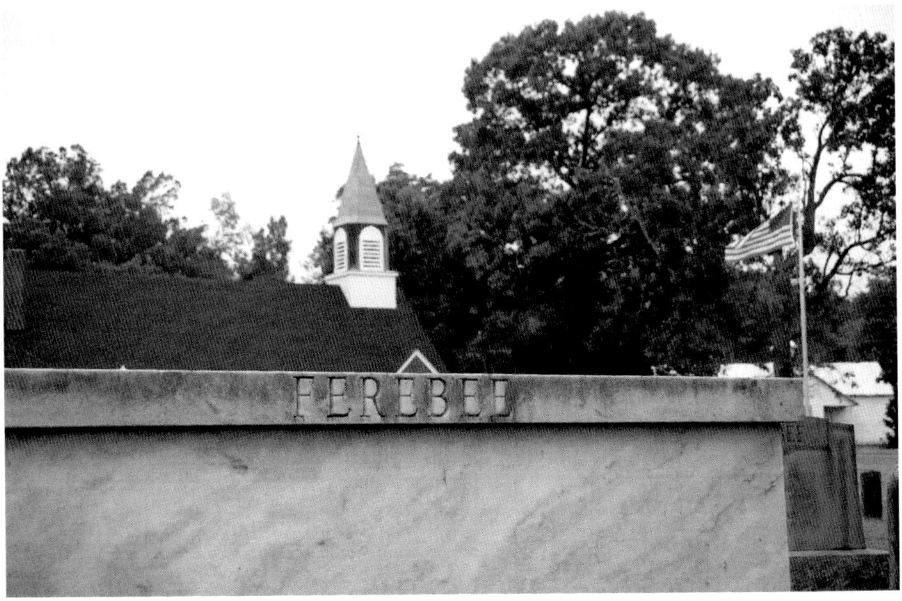


Ferebee family burial plot at Wesley Chapel Methodist Church. *Collection of Stephen Phillips.*

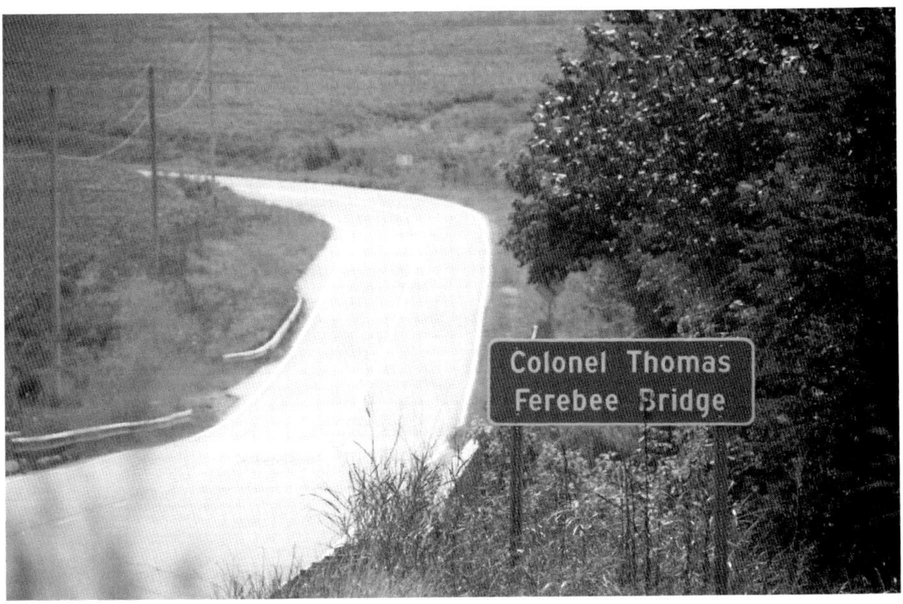


Bridge on U.S. Highway 64 named for Ferebee. *Collection of the author.*

attention in their backyards and saluted. The boy who had gazed up at planes over Davie County and changed history in one was honored by planes and a grateful nation.

Thomas Ferebee's contribution to history changed the twentieth century by ushering in the Atomic Age, not just for the United States but for the entire world. Warfare would never be the same. Little boys would now play war with toy airplanes and by making exploding noises, and the Cold War would be a standoff with the risks of another type of war looming from the skies. Of course, someone else could and would have been the bombardier if Tom had become a baseball player or stayed home to farm, but perhaps the outcome would have been different. The values and calm determination that controlled that steady hand were straight out of the farm fields and woods of Davie County, but they served the world. Boone crossed half a continent and Helper traveled the Western Hemisphere, but Ferebee soared around the world and left a mark like none other. Big stories can indeed begin in small places.

# Conclusion

So what of the small place where three stories began? Was there something special about the soil along the shores of Bear Creek or the place on the map in Davie County where three young men developed and left to aspire to greater things? While Helper spent his childhood and youth there, Boone arrived as a restless teenager and Ferebee knew it as home first as a college student who still hunted there. They may have come to the land at different stages of development, but it was the homeplace from which they all departed to answer the call of the bigger world. One can almost imagine three different young adult males lying on the ground in buckskin, cotton or denim and stargazing at the night sky, dreaming of what it held beyond what they knew. One would live to see Americans living in towns west of the Smoky Mountains for the first time, another would live to see trains and planes shrink the earth in transportation and the last would live to see man walk on the moon. Ney arrived as an adult with his glory days behind him, yet he learned to be a schoolteacher and make a contribution of a quieter type in life. The place also nurtured his learning curve and gave him peace at the end of his life. Amazingly, all four men lived long lives and died in old age, after having led very dangerous lives.

Bear Creek is still present, rather hidden from public view unless one slows down when crossing a bridge on Highway 64 over it, and a bit diminished in size like so many creeks in the area since water is often redirected upstream for irrigation. The little creek made the news in 1976 when the *Davie County Enterprise Record* Special Bicentennial Edition reported an oil spill from

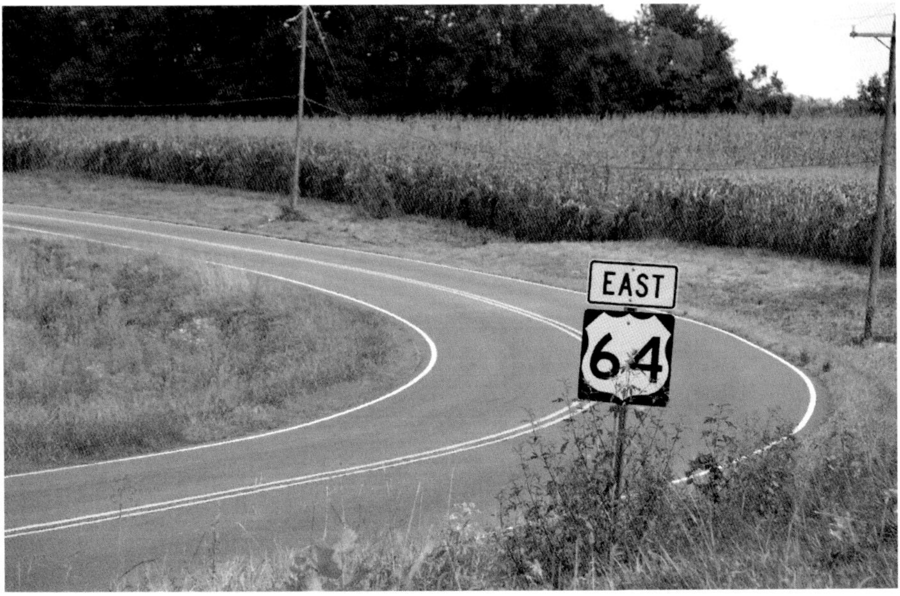


U.S. Highway 64 connects Davie County to the rest of the country and to history. *Collection of Stephen Phillips.*

Ingersoll-Rand after a week of heavy rain that caused a runoff lagoon at the factory to overflow into Bear Creek. It was promised that the problem would be addressed and corrected, but this serves as a distinctive example of twentieth-century technology (and ever-present weather) impacting a very old creek.

Highway 64, the modern version of the old road that connected farms, still winds its asphalt ribbon through Davie County. Interestingly, the last piece of U.S. Highway 64 between Lenoir in the mountains and North Carolina's east coast was straightened and finished between the community of Fork and the town of Mocksville in 1933, making old Davie County pathways the final link to be modernized between the western and eastern parts of the state. Interstate 40 now slices through Davie County (and appears as an artificial line of separation between the Boone/Helper farm and the Ferebee one on Highway 64) as it connects the North Carolina Atlantic coast at Wilmington to the Mojave Desert in Barstow, California. The gain of the interstate was speed; the loss is local sweet spots. As journalist and North Carolina native Charles Kuralt often said, "Thanks to the interstate highway system, it is now possible to travel across the country from coast to coast without seeing anything." Travelers speeding past rural

Davie County would do well to exit, slow down and observe where history-making began in the lives of three young men in three centuries on three miles of road by an old creek bed.

Does dirt or woods or water or air empower children to accomplishment? While it is difficult to prove a link between the physical environment and the human endeavor, it is hard to ignore that history makers have to come from somewhere, and these three came from the same three-mile stretch of land on Highway 64 where their historic markers line up like soldiers today. These strong individuals began their adult lives in Davie County countryside but changed the course of American history in three different centuries and very unique ways.

Is it just chance or a good place that produced them and still produces daring individuals who can be the game changers for another century? Men are shaped by their DNA but also by the environment that challenges their ability to survive and thrive. Those challenges can take the nature of tough city streets as well as woods. However, when conquering nature, as Boone and Ferebee both did in their later accomplishments, it seems important to have honed those skills first in a very natural setting. Colonial cities such as New York or Philadelphia could not have prepared Boone to trap, hunt or shoot, all skills that made it possible for him to survive the imposing mountains he had before him to cross.

The tougher issue is the formation of character. Is that shaped primarily by the physical obstacles to be overcome or the people who motivate one toward courage? Or is it molded by the beliefs that one holds to and then are held by? The answer is all three, and they are inseparable. People who live in a demanding terrain—more importantly when, as pioneers, they chose to subdue such a place—are by necessity brave. They both demonstrate and pass that strength of character on to their descendants. All three of the Davie County young men came from families who were early pioneers in the area.

Courage learned from the stimulus of a tough environment and strong people can manifest itself in various ways. The same willingness to take risks that prompted Boone to travel where no roads lay also prompted Helper to write controversial words and Ferebee to accept an assignment like none before it. That risk-taking ability is not formed by soft lives or easy paths. Boone's resistance from wilderness terrain mirrored Helper's family dynamics and Ferebee's failure to achieve his first goals in life. Perseverance is developed not in one crisis but repeated obstacles to overcome. Does that make Davie County a difficult place to live? Or is it the right mix of challenges met with help from a nurturing culture that encourages success?

Davie County is a place with deeply held values, rooted in the Bible preaching in its churches and the hearts of the hearers. The conservative politics reinforces honoring God and country and family. The culture runs on loyalty, something Helper did not understand. This place still produces principled and disciplined warriors and a steely resolve that can start here and go anywhere with a person.

One hero produced in a geographical area can be a fluke, a seemingly magical convergence of the best genes and a healthy environment. However, three distinctively different men who grew up on the same piece of land in the countryside seems to indicate that place plays a stronger role in human development than often acknowledged.

Ironically, the missing element in this story is any influence these native sons might have had on one another. The later ones no doubt knew about the previous ones, but the three Davie County men in this story did not directly impact one another, meaning the environment played a more important role than any did to one another. Nor could they have during their lifetimes. By sheer coincidence, nine years separated their lifetimes each time. This was the case with Boone's lifetime (he died in 1820) ending nine years before Helper's began (he was born in 1829). Nine years also separated the lives of Helper (who died in 1909) and Ferebee (born 1918), who died in 2000.

Somewhere growing up in Mocksville today is a child who was born in 2009, nine years after Thomas Ferebee died. Wonder what he or she will grow up to do in this century?

# Selected Bibliography


Brown, David. *Southern Outcast: Hinton Rowan Helper and the Impending Crisis of the South*. Baton Rouge: Louisiana State University Press, 2006.

Campbell, Richard H. *The Silverplate Bombers: A History and Registry of the* Enola Gay *and Other B-29s Configured to Carry Atomic Bombs*. Jefferson, NC: McFarland and Company, Inc., 2005.

Drake, Richard B. *A History of Appalachia*. Lexington: University of Kentucky Press, 2001.

Draper, Lyman C., and Ted Franklin Belue, eds. *The Life of Daniel Boone*. Mechanicsburg, PA: Stackpole Books, 1998.

Faragher, John Mack. *Daniel Boone: The Life and Legend of an American Pioneer*. New York: Henry Holt and Company, 1992.

Hairr, John. *North Carolina Rivers: Facts, Legends and Lore*. Charleston, SC: The History Press, 2007.

Harder, Robert O. *"The Three Musketeers of the Army Air Forces": From Hitler's Fortress Europe to Hiroshima and Nagasaki*. Annapolis, MD: Naval Institute Press, 2015.

Jones, Randell. *In the Footsteps of Daniel Boone*. Winston-Salem, NC: John F. Blair, 2005.

———. *Trailing Daniel Boone: Daughters of the American Revolution Marking Daniel Boone's Trail 1912–1915*. Winston-Salem, NC: Daniel Boone Footsteps, 2012.

Lefler, Hugh Talmadge, and Albert Ray Newsome. *North Carolina: The History of a Southern State*. Chapel Hill: University of North Carolina Press, 1954.

Morgan, Robert. *Boone: A Biography*. Chapel Hill, NC: Algonquin Books of Chapel Hill, 2007.

Niven, Penelope. *Old Salem: The Official Guidebook*. Winston-Salem, NC: Old Salem, Inc., n.d.

Smoot, J. Edward. *Marshal Ney: Before and After Execution*. Charlotte, NC: Queen City Printing Company, 1929.

Wall, James W. *History of Davie County in the Forks of the Yadkin*. Spartanburg, SC: Reprint Company, 1997.

Webb, James. *Born Fighting: How the Scots-Irish Shaped America*. New York: Broadway Books, 2004.

# Index

## S



## T



## U



## V



## W

# Y

# About the Author

Marcia Dollar Phillips, an educator for thirty-five years, currently works as museum educator at Old Salem and owns her own research business. She holds a master's in historic preservation from Eastern Michigan University.